101
Things
Every
KiD
Should Do
Growing
UP

Alecia T. Devantier

(a Kennedy Associates book)
foreword by Chris Cerf

SOURCEBOOKS, INC.
NAPERVILLE, ILLINOIS

Published by Sourcebooks, Inc.
P.O. Box 4410, Naperville, Illinois 60567-4410
(630) 961-3900
FAX: (630) 961-2168
www.sourcebooks.com

1-57071-862-8

Printed and bound in the United States of America
MV 10 9 8 7 6 5 4 3 2 1

Dedication
To K and Rose—
May your childhoods, and entire lives,
be complete.

Acknowledgments

There are many people who helped with this book in some way. To all of them, I owe a BIG thank-you!

To Carol Turkington, who believed in this idea from the first time I ran it by her: thank you for being my sounding board, and for sharing so many wonderful ideas.

To Dr. Dan Benjamin of the biology department at Central Michigan University: thank you for teaching me the finer points of turning a caterpillar into a beautiful butterfly.

To Janea Little at the Chippewa Nature Center: thank you for taking me on a moonlight hike in the middle of the afternoon.

To Cheryl Zylla: thank you for sharing your "sick socks."

To "The Sticker Lady," Denise Walton: thank you for teaching me how to scrapbook my memories.

To my agent, Bert Holtje: thank you for your help, support, and enthusiasm throughout this project.

To Jill Selleck, Pattie Curran, Carrie Stubbs, Kaysey Owczarzak, Megan Shaughnessy, Monica Bell, Kylene Everson, and Heather Miller, whose ideas were incorporated into entry No. 100. And, special thanks to everyone who submitted an idea; thank you for all your wonderful suggestions. I received many duplicate submissions, and I thank everyone who took the time to reply, whether your entry was used or not.

To my family. Kaylee, thank you for your inspiration, all your ideas, and playing nicely with Madeline when mommy was working. Madeline, thank you for all your smiles, hugs, and kisses. Robert, thank you for all your support, and always believing in my dreams.

And last, but definitely not least, thank you to everyone, parents, teachers, family, and friends, who helped to make my childhood complete.

Table of Contents

Foreword   xiii

Introduction   xv

1. Every kid should do something to make the world a better place.   1

2. Every kid should believe in things that can't be seen.   3

3. Every kid should go outside at dusk and stay there until it's dark, watching the stars come out.   6

4. Every kid should camp in the backyard.   9

5. Every kid should play in the bathtub until his skin wrinkles.   11

6. Every kid should play with play dough.   13

7. Every kid should receive notes of support, encouragement, or "just because."   16

8. Every kid should catch snowflakes on his tongue and eyelashes.   18

9. Every kid should write a thank-you note of gratitude to a relative or teacher.   20

10. Every kid should own one really fun piece of clothing.   22

11. Every kid should turn off the television for a weekend.   25

12. Every kid should eat homemade ice cream on a hot summer evening.   27

13. Every kid should help create a scrapbook of her childhood memories.   30

14. Every kid should go to a museum. 32

15. Every kid should build a gingerbread house and then get to eat it. 34

16. Every kid should spit watermelon seeds. 37

17. Every kid should do a "senior study." 39

18. Every kid should receive praise for who she is and what she has accomplished. 42

19. Every kid should have a favorite book or bedtime story. 45

20. Every kid should take a nighttime hike by the light of the moon. 48

21. Every kid should receive an award. 52

22. Every kid should make a special homemade present for Mom or Dad, Grandpa or Grandma. 54

23. Every kid should express creativity. 58

24. Every kid should learn how to swim. 61

25. Every kid should go for a ride in a small airplane. 64

26. Every kid should experiment with simple science projects. 66

27. Every kid should take music lessons. 69

28. Every kid should help bake a cake from scratch and then lick the frosting bowl. 72

29. Every kid should grow a vegetable garden. 75

30. Every kid should blow a bubble gum bubble until it pops. 79

31. Every kid should experience a family car trip. 82

32. Every kid should see a classic movie on the big screen. 85

33. Every kid should go to a parade. 87

34. Every kid should write in a journal. 90

35. Every kid should create a holiday keepsake. 93

36. Every kid should participate in a "-thon." 95

37. Every kid should possess a soft, cuddly stuffed animal, 97
that he is never forced to give up because he's "too old."

38. Every kid should have a collection. 100

39. Every kid should attend a live performance. 103

40. Every kid should let a fuzzy caterpillar crawl up her 106
arm, and then watch that caterpillar turn into a
butterfly.

41. Every kid should create a self-portrait. 109

42. Every kid should build a sand castle in the summer 111
and a snow fort in the winter.

43. Every kid should go on a factory tour. 114

44. Every kid should decorate the driveway. 118

45. Every kid should write a "memory letter" each year. 121

46. Every kid should explore other cultures. 123

47. Every kid should play dress-up. 126

48. Every kid should eat green eggs. 129

49. Every kid should ride a horse. 131

50. Every kid should have a treasure box. 133

51. Every kid should spend some time on a farm, even 135
for a short visit.

52. Every kid should be allowed the freedom to make choices, decisions, and mistakes. 138

53. Every kid should go to a fair, carnival, or amusement park. 141

54. Every kid should visit the place(s) where Mom and Dad grew up. 143

55. Every kid should get dressed up and go to a fancy dinner or restaurant. 145

56. Every kid should create a board game. 147

57. Every kid should have one outstanding teacher. 150

58. Every kid should write a letter to a favorite actor, athlete, or hero. 152

59. Every kid should have a pet. 154

60. Every kid should have a hobby. 156

61. Every kid should decorate her room according to the theme of her choice. 159

62. Every kid should take a trip to Washington, D.C. 162

63. Every kid should have a secret hideout. 166

64. Every kid should play classic games. 168

65. Every kid should run a lemonade stand. 171

66. Every kid should mark birthdays with a celebration. 174

67. Every kid should clown around. 177

68. Every kid should go to a family reunion. 179

69. Every kid should make a pizza. 182

70. Every kid should learn to appreciate the different 185
abilities of people.

71. Every kid should be taken for a "pajama ride." 188

72. Every kid should have a "get better" box. 190

73. Every kid should blow soap bubbles. 193

74. Every kid should spend some time alone with 195
each parent.

75. Every kid should build a model. 198

76. Every kid should go on a scavenger hunt. 201

77. Every kid should go to a baseball game with Grandpa. 203

78. Every kid should play with his food. 205

79. Every kid should see Mom or Dad laugh. 207

80. Every kid should make caramel apples. 209

81. Every kid should publish a book. 211

82. Every kid should have a best friend. 213

83. Every kid should experience the feelings of love, 215
safety, and security.

84. Every kid should participate in an extracurricular 218
activity.

85. Every kid should have a pen pal. 221

86. Every kid should have a personal library card. 224

87. Every kid should enjoy lazy summer days. 226

88. Every kid should experience the ocean.   228

89. Every kid should be given a camera to take pictures,   230
and the freedom to take whatever pictures she
wants to take.

90. Every kid should produce a video.   233

91. Every kid should experience the mystery of magic.   235

92. Every kid should go to summer camp.   239

93. Every kid should make a meal for the family.   241

94. Every kid should do chores around the house   244
without being paid.

95. Every kid should spend time alone.   247

96. Every kid should have an adventure.   250

97. Every kid should experience the beauty of nature.   252

98. Every kid should learn about the family's history.   254

99. Every kid should learn the value of money.   257

100. Every kid should have the opportunity to act like   260
a kid.

101. Every kid should have a dream for the future and   262
an adult who believes in that dream.

Checklist   265

About the Author   272

Foreword

What makes an ideal childhood? That's hard for me to say. I'm certainly no parenting expert. But from looking back on my life, I believe that when it comes to childhood experiences, every child should have the opportunity to share a common interest or hobby with a parent or other adult.

My dad loved baseball. He liked to write on the weekends, and we devised a way that he could write and yet also be with me to watch baseball. He would assign me to watch a game, and I had to call him if the Yankees had runners on second or third. He never missed the exciting moments. To me, it was really important—it was a wonderful way to find a way to be with your child.

As a child, I loved looking at the stars. A friend of my uncle was passionate about space and he gave me a great gift—the love of looking into the night sky, searching the stars. He was showing me something he loved, and he wanted to have someone to share it with. This developed into a lifelong interest, the result of an adult's excitement long ago. I still like looking at the stars.

It's important to spend time with your child, to share an experience equally. Find something you're passionate about, an age-appropriate common interest, and let your children see you participate in it. Invite them along as equals on the journey of discovery.

I think that generally where people might go wrong is to be condescending, to talk down to a child. Don't feel you "have" to do something with your child: "I have to introduce Johnny to music, because it's good for him." If you love music, that passion will be obvious.

Share your passion. That's what I try to do on my new kids' TV show, *Between the Lions* on PBS. I try to write things for kids that I find interesting. If it's boring to me, I figure it will be boring to a child. Kids need the chance to be silly and to laugh while they learn. I'm sharing my passion about reading and learning with a wide audience of children.

Reach out to a child and share your passion, too.

—Chris Cerf,
New York City

Introduction

I was excited for my oldest daughter as she finished preschool and prepared to go off to kindergarten. For her, it was a dream come true. At two, she'd stand at the living room window, wishing the school bus that passed by our house each morning and afternoon would stop for her. By three, she was packing books into her Tigger backpack so that she'd be all ready when it was her turn to go to school.

Now the time was at hand. As that first day of school approached, I found myself feeling more and more melancholy. Before long, she would be having all sorts of wonderful new experiences with her teacher and classmates: experiences that *I* wanted to share with her.

As we shopped for uniforms and a "grown-up" backpack, I thought about those activities and experiences that I wanted to share with her during her formative years—all the things she needed to do to have a *complete childhood*. I started to compile a list of all the things a child should do while growing up. And, while I had lots of ideas, I wanted input from other people who might have had different childhood experiences. So, I began polling friends and family members for their ideas; then I branched out to include friends of friends and family. Finally, I turned to the enormous power of the Internet, emailing people all over the country...and *101 Things Every Kid Should Do Growing Up* was born.

101 Things Every Kid Should Do Growing Up is a collection of 101 experiences every child should have. Wherever possible, I've tried to add practical suggestions to help you make the experience a reality for your child. The age range for the activities is three through twelve, but it's up to you to decide when your child is ready for the experience. For example, while a four-year-old could probably make a gingerbread house, it might be a much more successful and memorable experience with a ten-year-old. For some of the major suggestions, like a trip to Washington, D.C., you may want to make sure your child is old enough to get the most out of the experience.

Whenever you do them, have fun and enjoy making the most out of each one; after all, you're building a childhood! And who knows, maybe while you're at it you'll pick up a few things that you missed during your own childhood.

1

Every kid should do something to make the world a better place.

Encourage your child to try some of the following ways to make the world a better place:

- Hand out candy canes to all the store clerks you meet in December.

- Make a stack of Valentines and deliver them to a nursing home.

- Donate a portion of a weekly allowance to a charity.

- Mow the lawn, rake leaves, or shovel snow for someone who might need help.

- With the family, volunteer an afternoon at a soup kitchen.

- Cut fleecy fabric into 12–16" squares and donate them to local animal shelters to make the cages a little more comfortable.

- Collect hats and mittens, and restock the mitten boxes at local elementary schools.

- Help pick up trash in the park.

- Donate clean clothes or toys in good condition to a homeless shelter or a women's shelter.

- Draw a picture for the refrigerator of an elderly neighbor.

- Send homemade get-well cards to the children's ward at the local hospital.

- Plant some flowers or a tree.

Smile!

2

Every kid should believe in things that can't be seen.

Among the mystical, magical creatures that children know exist, but have yet to see, are "nap fairies" and "nap elves." Nap fairies and elves are creatures that live in an enchanted place somewhere between our world and Dreamland. They appear every afternoon after lunch, sprinkling fairy dust and leaving small gifts for napping boys and girls.

Help your child create a special drawstring bag for the nap fairy or elf, who can leave behind small rewards for your child.

1. Start with ¼ yard of magical material. Select a light- to medium-weight fabric decorated with stars, rainbows, a moon, glitter, or some other fairy- or elf-related motif.

2. Cut two 9" x 12" rectangles from the fabric.

3. On both pieces of fabric, fold in ½" on both edges along the 12" side, wrong sides together.

4. Iron down, and sew into place with a ¼" seam. You now have two 8" x 12" pieces of fabric.

5. Form a casing on each piece of fabric by folding down 1" on the 12" side, wrong sides together.

6. Sew in place.

7. Pin together the two pieces of fabric with the right sides facing.

8. Sew from the casing seam to ½" from the bottom. Sew along the bottom and along the other side to the casing seam.

9. Turn the bag right side out. Iron if necessary.

10. Cut a piece of ribbon or cording 24" long. Thread it through the casing on one side of the bag and back through the casing on the other side. Tie the ends together.

Note: It's much easier to thread the ribbon through the casing if you thread the ribbon through a large-eye, blunt needle or fasten a safety pin to the end of it.

Hang the bag on the outside doorknob of your child's bedroom door (be sure to leave the bag open) and the nap fairy or nap elf is sure to leave a special surprise before closing it! Favorite treats include a sticker, a few pennies, a small snack, or a small toy. And, of course, fairies and elves always leave behind a sprinkling of very fine glitter or several small, confetti stars, the perfect double for magic dust!

3

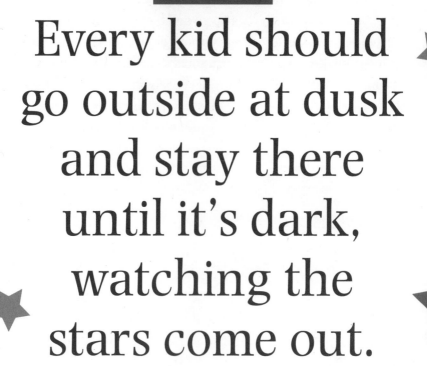

Every kid should go outside at dusk and stay there until it's dark, watching the stars come out.

Susan Shelly McGovern
Freelance writer
Shillington, PA

Lying beneath a blanket of stars on a warm evening, it's astounding to realize that those are the same stars that have fascinated people for centuries—the same stars they watched to determine when to plant their crops, the same stars they used to find their way home, the same stars that inspired stories, legends, and folklore.

Before heading out for a night under the stars, look up some of those legends and share them with your children. Take a star chart and highlight the stars in a few constellations, using a different color for each constellation. Help your child connect the stars. See if you can determine where the legends came from; does Ursa Major *really* look like a big bear?

Once you have located the constellations on paper, head outside armed with blankets, lounge chairs, and a chart of the heavens. When everyone is comfortable, locate the North Star. After you've established that place in the sky, try to find a couple of constellations. For best results, choose a moonless night for stargazing. If you live in an urban area, consider a trip to the country for optimal star viewing.

Bright moonlight isn't the best for star watching, but it's interesting to sit outside under the light of a full moon. As you sit there, remind your child that the moon doesn't generate any light—it's simply a big rock in the sky.

And don't forget to plan for some August stargazing. Each year, nature puts on a spectacular light show—the Perseid meteor shower. Depending on conditions, and how observant you are, you

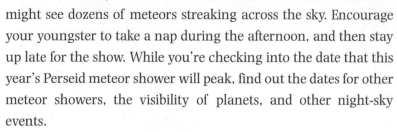

might see dozens of meteors streaking across the sky. Encourage your youngster to take a nap during the afternoon, and then stay up late for the show. While you're checking into the date that this year's Perseid meteor shower will peak, find out the dates for other meteor showers, the visibility of planets, and other night-sky events.

Keep that summer sky alive by bringing it inside. Help your child create constellations on the ceiling with plastic glow-in-the-dark stars, or wooden stars painted with a glow-in-the-dark paint. Attach them with a removable adhesive.

4

Every kid should camp in the backyard.

Camping out in the backyard is a great experience for kids, but it may not be practical or possible for city dwellers. But don't despair—if you don't have a backyard, try an indoor camp-out! You can create an outdoor experience in your own living room with just a few of the following fun suggestions:

- Simulate starlight by placing small, white, twinkle lights in artificial trees or plants.

- Attach glow-in-the-dark stars to the ceiling and walls with removable adhesive.

- Play a tape or CD of nighttime nature sounds.

9

- If you don't have an indoor pup tent, hang a blanket over a rope tied between two chairs—or camp "beneath the stars" on the carpet.

- Cook hot dogs on an indoor grill.

- Roast marshmallows over a gas stove.

- Make s'mores in the microwave (place a few pieces of chocolate and a marshmellow on a graham cracker, melt, top with another graham cracker, and enjoy!)

- Fill the bathtub, adding several drops of blue food coloring. Put on bathing suits and swim!

- Tell lots and lots of spooky stories.

5

Every kid should play in the bathtub until his skin wrinkles.

With bubbles or without, the bathtub is the perfect place to play, relax, and just be a kid. And, it's easier than you may think to turn your tub into a water wonderland. Here are some fun ideas.

Before your child climbs into the tub, make an armada of soap boats. To do this, cut masts or sails from recycled margarine-tub lids. Make small slits in the sails and attach them to bars of Ivory soap with round toothpicks. Float the soap boats in the tub.

Combine art time and bath time with washable finger paints. Using a muffin tin as a palette, squirt a small amount of white liquid hand soap or mild dish soap into each of the cups. Stir in several drops of food coloring until you get the right shade. Add cornstarch until the mixture is no longer runny. (Be sure to test paint on a small section of tile and tub as the food coloring may stain the grout, the tile, or the tub.)

Make mountains of bubbles by using a wire whisk or rotary eggbeater to beat up the bubbles.

Craft foam will stick to tub and shower walls when it's wet. Cut basic shapes in a variety of colors, and let your child decorate the tub and walls.

Use food coloring to create colorful bath water. Add several drops of one color to the front of the tub and several drops of a second color to the back of the tub. Watch the colored waters combine. Experiment with different color combinations.

Use tub time as a chance to play tic-tac-toe, play hangman, or practice spelling words. *Washable* children's craft markers wipe off *most* ceramic wall tile and other shower or tub walls. Again, test in a small inconspicuous area to make sure the marker can be easily removed without staining.

Using large cookie cutters as templates, cut colorful kitchen sponges into a variety of shapes. These are great not only for washing, but also for cleaning up the washable marker and finger-paint creations.

Complete the experience with a warm, oversized towel, fresh from the dryer!

6

Every kid should play with play dough.

Kaylee Devantier
Kindergarten student
Mt. Pleasant, MI

A childhood favorite for more than forty years, Play Doh was introduced to the public in 1956. Dressed in an artist's smock and beret, the Play Doh mascot "Play Doh Pete" first appeared on packages in 1960. Since then, more than two BILLION cans have been sold.

Originally available only in off-white, three other colors (red, blue, and yellow) were introduced the following year. Since then, Play Doh has been produced in a number of colors and scents, including glow-in-the-dark, gold, silver, shampoo, shaving cream,

Funshine Sunshine, Splurple, and Pinktastic. You can make your own version of this classic with just a few ingredients from your kitchen cupboards. You'll need:

Ingredients
Unsweetened drink mix powder
1 cup water
1 tbsp. vegetable oil
food coloring
½ cup salt
1 cup white flour

1, In a large, heavy saucepan over medium heat, dissolve the drink mix powder in water.

2. Stir in vegetable oil.

3. For more intense color, add several drops of food coloring.

4. Add salt and white flour to the saucepan. Stir. The mixture will be lumpy.

5. Stir constantly until the mixture becomes doughy and doesn't have any spots that look wet.

6. Turn the mixture onto the counter and let it rest until it's cool to the touch. Knead until smooth. Store in an airtight container. *Note: Even though this play dough has great color and scent, it's not edible.*

Edible Play Dough

Younger kids can get in on the fun with this great edible version. For easy cleanup, have your child create works of art on a sheet of waxed paper.

Ingredients

5 graham crackers

⅓ cup + 1 tbsp. peanut butter

honey (if desired)

1. Put the whole graham crackers in a plastic zip bag and crush them into a powder (this can also be done in a blender or a food processor).

2. In a bowl, combine the graham-cracker crumbs and the peanut butter with a spoon or by hand, and mix to a dough-like consistency.

3. If mixture is too dry, add a small amount of peanut butter or honey; if it's too moist, add more graham-cracker crumbs.

7

Every kid should receive notes of support, encouragement, or "just because."

Kids love surprises and they also love to get notes, just as long as they aren't being sent home from the teacher! So why not slip a note into a lunchbox, book bag, or coat pocket to wish your child good luck on that math test, or just to say hello?

Make the notes stand out. Use brightly colored papers and markers. Decorate the notes with stickers.

For lunchbox notes, why not write on a napkin instead of paper? Napkins featuring various themes and favorite animated and cartoon characters are available at party and speciality shops.

For pre-readers and early readers, use freehand drawings or computer clip art to create rebus notes, substituting pictures for words (e.g. I ♥ you).

Celebrate improved test scores, completion of a science project, or mastery of multiplication tables by enclosing a few gold foil–wrapped chocolate coins along with the note.

Send an invisible, mystery message. Using a white crayon, write a message on a piece of white cardstock. Attach a marker with instructions—reveal the message by gently coloring over the surface of the note with a marker.

Using your child's favorite stuffed animals or other toys, stage some silly photos. Take pictures of the animals playing, working on the computer, eating a snack, napping, or playing dress-up. After the film is developed, use a mailing label to add a caption or message to each of the pictures. To protect the picture, slip it into a zip-top bag, especially if you are going to put it into a lunchbox.

If your child has a computer class or access to email during the day, check with the teacher for permission to send a note or card via email.

Send a card, note, or postcard in the mail, just because.

8

Every kid should catch snowflakes on his tongue and eyelashes.

*"A snowstorm is always exciting to me.
I never know when I am going to
find some wonderful prize!"
– Wilson A. Bentley*

Wilson A. "Snowflake" Bentley was born in Jericho, Vermont in 1865. Using a special camera with a microscope attachment, Bentley took his first successful photograph of a snowflake in 1884. During his lifetime, Bentley documented more than five

thousand snowflakes, and discovered that no two were exactly alike. Shortly before his death in 1931, more than two thousand of his photos were published in *Snow Crystals*. For more information on Snowflake Bentley, check out the Caldecott-winning book, *Snowflake Bentley* by Jacqueline Briggs Martin.

If your child would rather catch a snowflake than read about one, you can improve your odds by taking a trip to Blue Canyon, California. With an average annual snowfall of more than 240 inches, it's the snowiest city in the United States. If a trip to Blue Canyon is out, consider these other snowy cities: Marquette, Michigan, with an average of 128.6 inches, Sault Sainte Marie, Michigan, at 116.7 inches, Syracuse with 111.6 inches, or Caribou, Maine, at 110.4 inches.

The record for snow in one twenty-four-hour period was set in 1921, when seventy-six inches covered Silver Lake, Colorado. The record U.S. snowfall during a one-year period is 1,122 inches, which fell on Rainier Paradise Ranger Station from July 1971 to June 1972.

Here's a great idea to help your child experience the beauty of snowflakes: cover a heavy piece of cardboard with dark felt or paper, and place the cardboard in the freezer until it's cold. To capture individual flakes, take the cardboard outside on a day when there are lots of snow flurries and little wind. Catch flakes on the cardboard. Use a magnifying glass to get an up-close look.

9

Every kid should write a thank-you note of gratitude to a relative or teacher.

Becki & Keith Dilley
Parents of sextuplets
Berne, IN

Most children learn at an early age that it's polite to write thank-you notes for the gifts they receive, even if the gift was a really hideous sweater, three sizes too big.

But what about those gifts we get that we carry with us throughout our lives—a favorite hobby, a love of reading, a feeling of compassion? Why is it that we don't send thank-you notes to the people who have given us truly precious gifts—the person who taught you to read or sparked an interest in science, or the coach who instilled patience and determination while showing you how to hit that ball out of the park? What about that relative, neighbor, or family friend who taught you how to knit, bake pies, or carve a model?

Talk to your children about these intangible, yet priceless gifts and help them understand just how important they are. Then arm your child with paper, crayons, markers, scissors, and stickers, and help craft thank-you notes for all these gifts. Younger children may need your help expressing just how much the gift has meant. Have your child share some specific examples. Your son can tell his teacher about the book he just finished reading. The former baseball coach would be thrilled to hear about the nine home runs your daughter hit last season.

While you're helping your child write thank-you notes, why not write a few of your own?

10

Every kid should own one really fun piece of clothing.

If your child doesn't own a really fun piece of clothing, you can help them create one. It's easier than you think to turn a T-shirt, sweatshirt, pair of jeans, baseball cap, pair of socks, or pair of canvas tennis shoes into a wearable work of art!

Buttons and beads come in just about every color, shape, and design imaginable. Sew on a few, or sew on a lot!

Sew or glue on ribbons or fringe to match, complement, or accessorize. Be sure to use glue that is permanent and machine washable when dry.

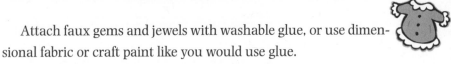

Attach faux gems and jewels with washable glue, or use dimensional fabric or craft paint like you would use glue.

With a large piece of heavy cardboard placed inside, a plain white T-shirt or sweatshirt becomes the perfect canvas for any young artist. Use fabric markers or fabric paints for a permanent work of art. For a changeable work of art, use *washable* craft markers. Follow the directions on the marker package for washing the shirt. Heavy coloring with the darker colors may leave faint color even after washing.

Cut patches in a variety of shapes and sizes from fabric. Use pinking shears or other decorative scissors to cut out some of the patches. Attach the patches to garments using an iron-on fusible adhesive.

Squeeze fabric or craft paint into a clean, recycled plastic jar. Dilute the paint with warm to hot tap water, mixing approximately two parts water to one part paint. Shake until the water and paint are mixed. Pour the mixture into a clean spray bottle. Hang the shirt on a clothesline or lay it on the ground. Spray the paint/water mixture onto the shirt one at a time. Mix up and spray additional colors as desired. Let the shirt air-dry for thirty to forty-five minutes, then toss it in the dryer on medium heat to finish drying it. After using the jar and spray bottle with paint, do not use it for food products.

Note: to reduce the risk of disappointment because a project doesn't turn out or last, wash and dry the garment *without* fabric softeners before decorating. And for best results, follow any manu-facturer's instructions or guidelines for the products you are using.

11

Every kid should turn off the television for a weekend.

Television is such a big part of American society that it is almost impossible to believe that it's only become a fixture in the last fifty years. TV is such a part of daily life that when the electricity goes out, many kids don't know what to do with themselves. Before the next power outage at your house, turn off the TV and find some other terrific ways to have fun:

- Get outside. Go for a walk, play ball, skip rope, blow bubbles, ride bikes, plant flowers, weed, fly a kite, or just enjoy the fresh air.

- Write a letter. Help your child write to a grandparent or family friend, sharing all the latest news and gossip.

- Play games. Get out the board games and play each of them at least once.

- Go on a road trip. Put your child to work making peanut butter sandwiches while you get the rest of the lunch ready. Pack a cooler and head off to explore a town you've never visited.

- Put on a talent show.

- Bake a big batch of cookies. Package up a couple dozen and deliver them to the neighbors or a local nursing home.

- Turn on some music and dance. Teach your child how to waltz, polka, or make up a dance of your own.

- Work on a family project. Build a birdhouse or feeder, make stepping stones for the garden, paint a table for the play room, build a child-size bookcase, or work on a vacation scrapbook.

Every kid should eat homemade ice cream on a hot summer evening.

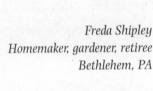

Freda Shipley
Homemaker, gardener, retiree
Bethlehem, PA

Those long, lazy summer evenings are the perfect time to whip up a batch of homemade ice cream using this simple recipe. **NO COMMERCIAL ICE CREAM MACHINE NEEDED.**

You'll need:

Ice Cream Maker Ingredients

Small coffee can with plastic lid, washed and dried

Duct tape

2 lbs crushed ice

Rock salt

Large coffee can with plastic lid (washed and dried)

Ice Cream Ingredients

1 cup whipping cream

1 cup milk

½ cup sugar

1 tsp. vanilla

Optional: flavoring extracts, chocolate syrup, food coloring, chocolate chips, chopped candy bars or nuts, crushed cookies, fruit puree, brownies or cake (broken into small pieces), or candy sprinkles

1. Combine the whipping cream, milk, sugar, and vanilla in a small clean coffee can.

2. Add flavoring extracts or chocolate syrup. Food coloring can be added to create really cool colors.

3. Put the lid on the can and seal with duct tape.

4. Place a layer of ice on the bottom of a large coffee can. Put the small can inside the large can, on top of the ice.

5. Pack ice and rock salt around the small can, alternating layers of ice and salt.

6. Place the lid on the large can and shake the can or roll it on the ground. Keep it moving!

7. Drain off melted water and replace the ice and salt as necessary.

8. After about fifteen minutes, rinse the outside of the small can with cold water, open, and stir in one or more of the optional items, if desired.

9. Replace the small lid and re-tape. Drain water, add ice and salt, and replace the large lid. Shake for fifteen to twenty more minutes.

10. Rinse the outside of the small can with cold water before opening. For hard ice cream, place the can in the freezer until the desired consistency is achieved.

11. Enjoy! Any leftover ice cream should be stored in a plastic, freezer-safe container.

13

Every kid should help to create a scrapbook of her childhood memories.

Best friends...1st day of school...Dance recitals...Field trips...
School plays...Little League...Childhood pets...Summer vacations
...Halloween costumes...The precious memories of childhood.

Help your child to preserve these memories by working together to make a scrapbook. Keep the memories alive by including information about the who, what, when, and where of each picture.

In addition to a scrapbook with photos, you can use newspaper and magazine articles and clippings to document fashion trends, hairstyles, popular television shows, movies, music, automobile styles, current events, and major news stories. Newspaper clippings will hold up better if they are photocopied onto acid-free paper. Be sure to date any articles or clippings. When your children are older, they will have a wonderful scrapbook to share with their children. They'll be able to show how people dressed, how much (or little) things cost, and headlines from the major news stories from their childhood.

The key to a long-lasting scrapbook is in the supplies. To create a scrapbook that will last for years and years, use only acid-free materials in your scrapbook: paper, stickers, pens, glues, and adhesives.

When it comes to designing a scrapbook page, there really aren't any rules. If *you* like it, use it. You are, after all, cataloging your pictures and the memories that go along with them. Scrapbook experts do suggest that you resist the urge to crop your pictures too much, leaving only the subject of the photo. Years from now, it will be interesting to look back at the landscape, cars, people, and other "background" items you might have wanted to crop from the picture.

14

Every kid should go to a museum.

Antique cars...Paperweights...Relics from lost civilizations...Dinosaur bones and skeletons...Vintage aircraft...Clothing, toys, and household items from bygone days...Mummies...Artwork and photographs.

Collections of wonderful things await your child at a museum. It's just a matter of matching the collection with your child's special interest! If your child is fascinated with cars, don't be disappointed if a dinosaur display draws yawns—even if it's one of the best exhibits in the country. And make sure that your child is the right age to visit a special "kids'" museum—not too young to understand the exhibits nor too old to enjoy the hands-on activities.

If you're planning to make a special trip to visit a museum, stock up beforehand on maps and information—and plan, plan, plan! Large museums usually offer more than you can possibly enjoy in a single day trip, especially if you're traveling with small children. Look through the brochures with your child to find out what the museum has to offer, and then plan what you would like to see. Since your time will be limited, create a list of favorites and then prioritize. Remember to plan frequent breaks into your schedule. Everyone will enjoy the museum experience more if they're rested and well fed.

If possible, read a story or two related to the exhibit before you visit. For example, if your local museum is hosting a special exhibit of French history, spend a few nights at bedtime reading *Marie Antoinette: Princess of Versailles* in The Royal Diaries series. Your child will have a real sense of French history *before* hitting the museum, and be much better able to appreciate the artifacts on view.

Once you're there, if the museum allows, touch, touch, touch! Kids have a much better time when they can get involved with the exhibits, which is why so many places feature "Please touch!" shows for youngsters. Consider making your child's first museum trip a visit to a hands-on museum. Everyone—including you—is guaranteed to have fun.

Don't forget to stop in at the museum store after your visit. Pick up a book or kit with activities that will reinforce the things you experienced.

15

Every child should build a gingerbread house and then get to eat it!

Pattie Curran
Social worker/stay-at-home mom
Danville, VA

There's something magical about gingerbread houses. Maybe it's the shredded-wheat thatched roof, the sugar-wafer shutters, or the

34

cotton-candy smoke wafting out of the chimney. Perhaps it's the pretzel-stick split-rail fence or the sugar-cone pine trees and marshmallow snowmen that dot the landscape. Whatever it is, take an afternoon and make some magic with a child, and when you're done, pour a couple of cold glasses of milk and dig in!

Gables

To create a masterpiece in your own kitchen, start by breaking a whole graham cracker in half, then cut along the diagonal with a sharp knife. This will form the gables of the house. (Note: graham crackers are somewhat difficult to cut. Save any broken pieces to use in other places.)

Mortar

Now you'll need to prepare a batch of "mortar" (also known as royal icing).

Ingredients
1½ tbsp. meringue powder
¼ tsp. cream of tartar
2 cups sifted powdered sugar
3 tbsp. lukewarm water

Using an electric mixer, beat together all of the ingredients until you can use a spoon or butter knife to pull up peaks that are stiff

35

and maintain their shape. This takes five to ten minutes. Royal icing dries out quickly, so place a piece of plastic wrap on the surface of the icing when it is not in use!

Construct the House

Using the mortar, attach the graham-cracker gables to two of the sides of the house. For extra stability, apply a layer of mortar to the entire back of the side and gable. Let the frosting harden for a few minutes. Mortar the sides of the house together. Allow the icing to set up for a few minutes before attaching the graham-cracker roof. If you plan to eat the house as soon as construction is complete, you do not need to let the icing dry completely. It only needs to be firm enough to hold the pieces together.

House Decorations

Using icing to hold things in place, decorate the house with gumdrops, assorted hard candies, candy canes and candy sticks, chocolate chips, colored sugars, candy sprinkles, coconut, marshmallows, sugar cones, licorice laces, licorice bites, licorice twists, pretzel sticks, cookies, and cereals.

16

Every kid should spit watermelon seeds.

There's just nothing like spitting watermelon seeds for letting a kid feel really free! Jason Schayot holds the record; on August 12, 1995, he spat a watermelon seed seventy-five feet, two inches!

Of course, the bigger the watermelon, the more seeds there are for spitting—so your kids would have had fun with the largest watermelon on record, a 262-pounder grown by Tennessee's Bill Carson in 1990.

The United States is the fourth-largest producer of watermelons in the world, and watermelons are grown in forty-four of the fifty states—so you shouldn't have trouble finding a big green fruit for your kids to practice on!

Once you get your watermelon home, try setting up some contests for your kids to enjoy:

- Try spitting seeds into a coffee can at different distances—the farthest seed gets a prize!

- Draw a line in the dust and see who can spit the first seed over the line.

- Place a child on either end of a square of sand or dirt. Draw a line in the middle, and have one child spit over the line. Draw a new line where that seed lands. Now have the second child spit a seed over *that* line; if successful, draw a new line marking that seed.

Tip: the secret to spitting is to curl the tongue as the seed is spit— and choose the biggest possible seed for the longest distance!

17

Every kid should do a "senior study."

Most children have a hard time believing that their parents or grandparents were ever children. They probably don't know that Grandpa played tuba in the marching band or that Grandma was a track star who had the lead in every school play.

There are a million stories about your parents that your child has never heard. In fact, there are probably some that *you* have never heard. Your child can collect and save all these stories and memories for future generations by doing a "senior study."

To prepare for a "senior study," tell your child some facts about their grandparents' life: place and date of birth, information about parents and siblings, and anything else you might know. Help your child to come up with some basic questions about the grandparent's childhood. These might include:

- What was the town you grew up in like?

- Who was your best friend growing up? What was that person like?

- Where did you hang out?

- What is the craziest thing you ever did in school?

- What were your favorite things to do as a child? (hobbies, sports, etc.)

- What was your favorite subject in school? Why? Least favorite? Why?

- What was your favorite movie? Book? Food? Television or radio show?

- What was your first job?

- What was the scariest thing that ever happened to you growing up?

Help your child research some of the major historic events that took place in the grandparent's lifetime. With that information, help your child develop some questions to ask about those events and how they affected the grandparent personally.

Next, have your youngster create and send a special invitation asking the grandparent for an interview. If possible, tape-record or videotape the interview for posterity. Shortly after the interview, help your child compile all the information and write up the stories. And if you can, gather childhood photos of the grandparent and include them in the "study."

Note: if your child can't interview a grandparent, try another family member or friend who's about the same age as the grandparent.

18

WAY TO G

Every kid should receive praise for who she is and what she has accomplished.

great job!

Tina Moreau-Jones
Associate Pastor
Mt. Pleasant, MI

The next time your child brings home a great paper, don't just say how proud you are; *show it*—with some all-star recognition.

Recognize your super star. Kids of all ages like to have their hard work noticed, especially by Mom or Dad. Gold stars and stickers are a terrific way to let your child know that you are proud of her performance. But don't save the gold stars only for 100 percent papers—why not acknowledge that hour spent studying for the spelling test, even if the score was only a 78 percent?

Display papers, artwork, certificates, and complimentary notes from the teacher on the refrigerator or on a bulletin board dedicated specifically to your child's work. Consider installing an individual bulletin board for each child. Update the refrigerator or bulletin board with new papers and artwork often.

Each Friday, sit down with your child and go through all school papers and artwork from the week. Have your child select a favorite paper or piece of artwork, and frame it. Display it proudly in your house. Change the paper weekly.

Share the good news. Most children bring home more papers than you could possibly ever save. After reviewing the papers with your child and displaying them on the refrigerator or bulletin board for a while, select several good papers or examples of artwork to send to grandparents, aunts and uncles, and other close family friends. To share exceptional school papers or artwork, make a color copy.

Let the whole world know how proud you are of your child. Print-your-own bumper stickers and window decal kits are available at most office- or computer-supply stores. Make a decal for the rear window of your car, and tell the world that you have the science-fair winner, a tennis whiz, or just a super kid on board.

you're a winner!

SUPER KID!

congratulations!

GREAT GAME!

19

Every kid should have a favorite book or bedtime story.

Who could forget that well-loved, dog-eared book that both you and your child could recite from memory?

If your child doesn't have a favorite book, stop by your local bookstore or library and pick up a few Caldecott Medal winners. First awarded in 1938, the Caldecott Medal is given each year to the artist of the best American children's picture book published during the previous year. The last ten Caldecott Medal winning books are:

- 2001 – *So You Want to Be President?* illustrations by David Small, text by Judith St. George

- 2000 – *Joseph Had a Little Overcoat*; text and illustrations by Simms Taback

- 1999 – *Snowflake Bentley*; illustrations by Mary Azarian, text by Jacqueline Briggs Martin

- 1998 – *Rapunzel*; text and illustrations by Paul O. Zelinsky

- 1997 – *Golem*; text and illustrations by David Wisniewski

- 1996 – *Officer Buckle and Gloria*; text and illustrations by Peggy Rathmann

- 1995 – *Smoky Night*; illustrations by David Diaz, text by Eve Bunting

- 1994 – *Grandfather's Journey*; illustrations by Allen Say, text edited by Walter Lorraine

- 1993 – *Mirette on the High Wire*; text and illustrations by Emily Arnold McCully

- 1992 – *Tuesday*; text and illustrations by David Wiesner

Each year since 1922, the Newbery Medal has been awarded to the author of the best American children's book published during the previous year. Read one of these books aloud *with* your older child.

The last ten Newberry Medal winning books are:

- 2001 – *A Year Down Yonder* by Richard Peck

- 2000 – *Bud, Not Buddy* by Christopher Paul Curtis

- 1999 – *Holes* by Louis Sachar

- 1998 – *Out of the Dust* by Karen Hesse

- 1997 – *The View from Saturday* by E.L. Konigsburg

- 1996 – *The Midwife's Apprentice* by Karen Cushman

- 1995 – *Walk Two Moons* by Sharon Creech

- 1994 – *The Giver* by Lois Lowry

- 1993 – *Missing May* by Cynthia Rylant

- 1992 – *Shiloh* by Phyllis Reynolds Naylor

20

Every kid should take a nighttime hike by the light of a full moon.

Carol Turkington
Writer
Mohnton, PA

The next time a full moon and favorable weather coincide, head out with your child for a hike by the light of the moon to discover a world that's just waking up.

Nighttime is full of sounds that may be unfamiliar to many children, and some of these sounds can be very scary—hoots, caws, squeaks, hisses, screams, scratching, and rustling. To prepare your child for the things you'll hear on your hike, listen to a tape or CD of nighttime nature sounds. Talk about the sounds that you hear. Here are some more tips to enjoy these late-night outings:

- For the best animal sightings, head out about an hour before dark.

- Be prepared for the weather, especially in the fall and winter. Temperatures can drop off very quickly when the sun goes down.

- Bring along a flashlight, but resist the urge to use it to light your way. Allow your eyes to adjust to the dark, and you'll actually be able to see further than you would be able to with the flashlight. If your children insist on using a flashlight, cover the lens with a piece of red film, cellophane, or plastic wrap. The red light will be less disturbing to your eyes and to any animals. (Some animals, raccoons for example, don't see light in the red spectrum).

- If you want to see or hear animals on your hike, it's very important to be quiet. Nighttime air holds more moisture than daytime air; noises are amplified and travel further.

- What you see or hear during your hike will depend, in part, upon where you live or hike. If you have a nature center, zoo, or college in your area, ask someone what to look for, what to listen for, and where to hike in your area. Whomever you speak with might also be able to offer other suggestions for a successful experience.

- In the spring, if you hike near a swampy area, listen for the mating calls of tree frogs. You might also hear owls, rails, or woodcocks.

- In the summer, you'll see and hear bugs. So that you offer less of a snack, wear long sleeves and long pants, and spray with repellent.

- In June and July, you might hear or see baby squirrels, raccoons, or skunks. Born in April or May, they are taking their first nighttime hikes as well.

- For reasons unknown to naturalists and scientists, the firefly population is decreasing. If your child wants to catch a few fireflies in a jar, insist that they be released after an up-close look.

- If you should happen to meet up with a skunk on your hike, be quiet and still until it has gone on its way. Skunks spray when they are scared by noise or fast movements.

- In the fall, you may see or hear animals preparing for winter. Everyone is eating more. Many of the spring babies are now grown, and they are setting up homes of their own. The September harvest moon and the hunter moon of October are beautiful for moonlight hikes.

- If you're brave enough to venture out for a hike by the full moon during the winter, you might be lucky enough to hear the calls of great horned owls, who court during this time of year.

- Most important, take all necessary safety precautions, and heed any warnings about bears, wolves, coyotes, or other predatory animals.

21

Every kid should receive an award.

Whether it's a trophy or medallion, a blue ribbon, or an embossed certificate worthy of framing, every child should receive a reward for hard work and a job well done—especially for the child who worked hard but didn't come out on top. Present an award or certificate to your child for getting a 100 percent on a math test, for sharing and playing nicely with younger brothers and sisters, or for just being a terrific kid! Show your child that he or she is a winner in your eyes by presenting an award for a job well done:

- Certificates: fancy, official-looking certificates are available at most office-supply stores and educational or teachers' supply stores. You can also make personalized certificates on your home computer. For an extra-special achievement, put the certificate into an inexpensive frame decorated with appropriate buttons and trinkets.

- Ribbons: buy a short piece of satin ribbon from your local fabric or craft store. Cut an inverted V into the bottom, and with a metallic paint pen, record the event on the ribbon: "Terrific Tumbler," "Soccer Champ," "Super Soloist," or "No. 1 Speller."

- Trophy: you can make almost any occasion memorable by presenting your superstar with a trophy. Buy a small theme-related trophy and have it engraved with the event and the date. For example, you could get a small trophy with a baseball player to celebrate a first home run, or a gold cup for all the time and hard work put into a science-fair project.

- Theme meal or awards banquet: celebrate participation in a spelling bee with a big bowl of alphabet soup. For fun, decorate the table with small cards spelling out the items on the table, for example, "p-l-a-t-e," "g-l-a-s-s," "c-h-a-i-r," and "s-a-l-a-d." Remember a basketball season with a dinner of spaghetti and miniature hamburger "basketballs"; finish with a round cake frosted basketball orange; black licorice laces add details. Present your child with a basketball certificate made from orange craft foam. Mark the last day of swimming lessons with a meal featuring fish sticks; for an extra-special dessert, serve blue gelatin complete with gummy fish. Hand out a tropical fish award made out of colorful craft foam.

22

Every kid should make a special homemade present for Mom or Dad, Grandpa or Grandma.

Norma Testa
Executive Director
Wilmington, DE

There's nothing that parents and grandparents love more than receiving a gift made by their child or grandchild. There's something very special about these gifts, created with infinite care and love—and children enjoy creating gifts for the special adults in their lives.

Crafting with young children not only helps them develop skills, it also teaches them at an early age that some of the best presents don't come from a store—they're made with hands and hearts. There are many simple projects children can do with just a bit of adult assistance so that the gift is truly their own creation. Here's a fun way to help your child create something really special.

Handmade Art Work

Help your youngster select a special frame and cut a piece of heavy paper or cardstock to fit the frame. Have your child create a work of art on the paper or cardstock. Depending on talents and preferences, your child may choose to draw a picture, write a short story, create a poem, or make a collage. For younger children, you can photocopy a picture from a coloring book onto heavy paper or cardstock, reducing or enlarging as needed to fit the frame. The possibilities are endless. Regardless of what your child decides to make, be sure that the masterpiece is signed and dated.

Plaster of Paris Paperweight

An inexpensive package of plaster of paris can be used to make great paperweights. Mix up a batch according to the manufacturer's directions on the package. Follow any instructions or precautions on the package for preparing the mold and hardening times. For easier removal, use a rubber or flexible-plastic mold. Your child can paint the finished item using acrylic craft paint. For younger children, cut a damp kitchen sponge into squares for easier "painting." Seal with several coats of clear acrylic spray. Cut a thin piece of felt the same size and shape as the bottom of the paperweight and glue it in place.

Bread Dough Art

A simple batch of bread dough can capture memories for a lifetime!

Ingredients

1 cup all-purpose flour
½ cup salt
½ cup warm water

1. Mix together flour and salt; stir in water.

2. Let your child work the mixture into a smooth dough.

3. Roll the dough between two pieces of waxed paper until it is about ¼" thick.

4. Remove the top piece of waxed paper and turn the dough onto a foil-lined cookie sheet.

5. Use a plastic food-storage container slightly larger than your

child's hand to cut a circle or square in the dough; remove excess.

6. Lightly dust the top of the dough with a small amount of flour. Have your child press a hand into the dough, gently yet firmly. If necessary, reshape with the plastic container.

7. Set the cookie sheet in a warm, dry place and let it dry for twelve hours.

8. After twelve hours, carefully turn the plaque over and use a toothpick to "write" your child's name and the date on the back.

9. Let it dry bottom side up for twelve hours; after twenty-four hours, the plaque can be dried in a *warm* oven. Turn it over several times while baking so that it will dry evenly. This may take up to twelve hours. (Note: baking slowly reduces the chance that air pockets will form in the plaque).

10. Once the plaque is dry, your child can paint it using acrylic craft paint. Seal with a coat of clear acrylic spray.

23

Every kid should express creativity.

Creativity comes in many forms: paintings and drawings, collages, sculptures, stories, poetry, song, dance, and others. Be prepared ahead of time for when creativity strikes—gather a Creativity Box of supplies. The Creativity Box could include any of the following:

- Child-safe scissors

- Crayons, markers, and colored pencils

- Paper: white, colored, and lined

- Lightweight cardboard

- Old magazines

- Craft glue

- Yarn and embroidery floss

- Ribbons

- Fabric scraps and felt

- Pom-poms

- Buttons and beads

- Dimensional fabric/craft paints

- Clay

There are a lot of fun and unique ways to spark creativity in your child. Try these ideas.

Use Music as Inspiration

Play a selection of music and have your child create a work of art representing the feelings it evoked—draw a picture, create a collage, write a poem, make up a dance, or create a musical composition based on the piece. Experiment with different types of music, such as salsa, classical (everything from Ravel's Bolero to Mozart, Bach, and Beethoven), lullabies, marches, and even some classic rock 'n' roll.

Take a Trip to the Closest Art Museum

If that's not possible, look through art books for reproductions or photos of famous works. This is not only a terrific way to introduce your child to classic works of art, it's also a wonderful way to introduce various styles of painting, sculpting, or other art. Encourage your child to experiment with the different styles you see.

Finish the Story

Check out, from the library, a book that your child hasn't read. Read the first half of the story, and then have your child create an original ending. After it's finished, compare it to the real ending.

Create Your Own

Help your child cut out pictures from a variety of colorful catalogs. Toss them in a hat, and each of you select four or five pictures. Each person then takes a turn and makes up a story using the pictures.

Make Some Art

Gather several children together, and get out the Creativity Box. One by one, deal each child an item from the box. When each child has five or six items, have each of them create a picture using only the materials they have. Suggest a category, such as "aliens from space" or "crazy critters."

24

Every kid should learn how to swim.

A big, backyard pool or a local swimming hole is the perfect place to cool off on a summer afternoon—if you know how to swim. Don't let your child be left on the shore—arrange for swimming lessons *before* the weather warms up.

After your child has mastered the basics, you can reinforce those skills with some fun competitions. Toss a few large foil-wrapped potatoes, colored golf balls, or coins into the pool and encourage your child to retrieve as many as possible. Be sure to provide a swim mask or goggles, if necessary. And don't forget, the more the merrier—dive in and join your child in some aquatic fun!

You might want to dress your child for the occasion with a new swimsuit. If you have a hard time finding a new suit because your child is learning to swim in the dead of winter, jazz up last year's suit by sewing on a few waterproof buttons, sequins, or patches. Of course, a brand-new beach towel is essential for completing the ensemble. With a few supplies, you and your child can create a colorful, personalized beach towel: (Note: before beginning, practice on an old towel.)

What you'll need:

Ingredients

Large white towel
Large foam craft stamps
Foam brushes, one for each color
Fabric paints, in a variety of colors
Paper plates, one for each color
Cotton swabs

1. Wash and dry the towel. (Don't use fabric softener!)

2. Squirt some fabric paint onto a paper plate.

3. Using a foam brush, apply a thick, even coat of paint to the stamp.

4. Use a cotton swab to clean any excess paint out of the cut-out or detail areas on the stamp. For best results, use a stamp that does *not* have a lot of detail.

5. Press the stamp firmly and evenly onto the towel.

6. Repeat as desired.

7. Follow manufacturer's instructions for setting the paint and laundering the finished item.

Tip: can't find foam stamps? Create your own! Cut simple designs out of thick craft foam, and use heavy-duty craft glue to attach the shapes to blocks of wood.

25

Every kid should go for a ride in a small airplane.

Lou Ballance
Handyman
Goodrich, MI

Tales of Amelia Earhart and Charles Lindbergh have always delighted children, prompting dreams of taking to the air. Now, thanks to the Experimental Aircraft Association (EAA) "Young Eagles" program, kids between the ages of eight and seventeen can turn dreams into reality by going for a ride in a small airplane at *no charge*. They can experience the indescribable feeling of taking off for the first time, the exhilaration of flight, and the bumpiness of a perfect landing.

Since its launch in July 1992, the Young Eagles program has given wings to more than 650,000 children. It's the program's goal to introduce one million kids to the joy of flying by 2003—the 100th anniversary of the Wright brothers' flight near Kitty Hawk, N.C. All participants will have their names entered into the world's largest logbook.

If your child is an avid aviator, and you live near the Wittman Regional Airport in Oshkosh, WI, check out the EAA AirVenture. This annual convention offers visitors the opportunity to see classic and antique aircraft, warbirds, commercially manufactured planes, ultralights, acrobatic aircraft, and experimental airplanes up close. Visitors also have the chance to see spectacular planes and stunts during the daily air show.

For more information about EAA AirVenture, the Young Eagles program, or to make the dream of flight a reality for your child, contact the Experimental Aircraft Association in Oshkosh, WI (877-806-8902 or www.eaa.org/youngeagles).

26

Every kid should experiment with simple science projects.

Who says science can't be fun? The results of these simple projects will excite your kids, even if they don't understand the theory behind them yet.

Instant Volcano

Using a funnel, put a tablespoon or two of baking soda into a small, clean, dry plastic bottle. Use fresh baking soda for best results. Place the bottle in the kitchen sink or bathtub and slowly add up to a cup of white vinegar until it foams out of the mouth of the bottle (large bottles may need more vinegar). Add several drops of food coloring for a colored volcano. For an extra-foamy volcano, add a squirt of liquid dish soap before adding the vinegar. Consider having young children wear eye protection in case they get too close to the volcano, especially if you add the dish soap.

Scuba Divers

Fill a clean, glass jar almost full with club soda or seltzer water. Add several raisins to the jar, and watch them scuba dive!

Rubber Egg

Put a hard-boiled egg into a clean mayonnaise or canning jar. Add enough white vinegar to the jar to cover the egg. Carefully change the vinegar every couple of days. Continue to soak the egg in vinegar until the shell has dissolved (this may take a week or more). Remove the egg from the vinegar and let it dry. You now have a rubber egg that will actually bounce. Be careful not to drop the egg from too far up, as it will break apart. Try the same thing with a fresh (uncooked) chicken or turkey leg bone. Wash the bone well before placing it in the jar. After about a week you'll have a flexible bone; you might even be able to tie it into a knot.

Storm Warning

To tell whether a thunderstorm is getting closer to your house or moving away from you, count the number of seconds between a flash of lightning and a crack of thunder. Do this for several sets of lightning and thunder. If the number is getting smaller, the storm is moving closer; if the number gets larger, it is moving away. To estimate how far away the storm is, divide the number of seconds by five to get an approximate distance in miles.

Celery Veins

Fill a mayonnaise or canning jar with water. Mix in several drops of food coloring. Put a freshly cut stalk of celery, leaves and all, into the colored water. Leave the celery in the water for several hours, checking on it occasionally. After several hours, the veins of the celery will become the color of the water. Try the same thing with a freshly cut white carnation; the fresher the carnation, the better the results.

Cricket Temperature

Sit outside on a hot summer evening and listen to the crickets. Count the number of chirps in a fifteen-second time period, add forty, and you have the approximate temperature (in Fahrenheit).

27

Every kid should take music lessons.

Pecking out "Twinkle, Twinkle, Little Star" on the keyboard or squawking out a scale on the clarinet—ah, the joys of childhood music lessons! Until it's time for music lessons, help your child have fun making and playing a gourd rattle.

Gourds are easy to grow, or you can buy some at a market in late summer or early autumn. A long season of drying in the warm sun and wind is the best for gourds. In colder climates, you can speed up the process with a warm oven. Be sure the gourd is completely dry before cutting, or it will wrinkle. Once you've dried your gourd, you can make a rattle! Here's how.

You'll need:

Ingredients

1 dried gourd any shape or size, but hard
Seeds from the gourd, pebbles, or beans
Dowel or stick—6" long and the width of neck of the gourd in
diameter, if necessary
Twine or heavy string
White glue
Acrylic paints, in a variety of colors
Clear sealer

1. Parent: with a knife, cut off the narrow end of the gourd; if the neck is long enough, leave most of it on for a handle.

2. Child: with a narrow spoon, scoop out the seeds and membrane inside the gourd. Save the seeds for the rattle.

3. Dry the gourd in the hot sun or oven at a low even temperature.

4. When dry, fill the gourd with seeds, beans, or pebbles.

5. If the gourd end is long enough for a handle, reattach it with white glue.

6. If not, you can use a dowel rod for the handle. To make, place glue on one end of the dowel and insert it in the neck of the gourd. Dry. Dip the twine in white glue and wrap it firmly around the dowel and up the gourd about ½".

7. Using acrylic paints, create a colorful design on the gourd; when dry, spray with a clear sealer to protect the finish.

28

Every kid should help bake a cake from scratch and then lick the frosting bowl.

Julie Bradford
Mother
Southampton UK

With the introduction of packaged cake mixes more than fifty years ago, baking cakes from scratch oftentimes became a thing of the past. Using a mix, cakes could be made quicker, and in many cases cheaper, than they could ever be made from scratch. Considering that packaged cake mixes have been around for more than two generations, most kids have never made a cake any other way.

The next time that rain cancels your afternoon plans, take a step back in time with your child and make a cake from scratch—and of course, a big bowl of homemade frosting to finish it off. When you're done, grab a couple of spoons and lick the bowl clean.

White Cake

Ingredients
2 cups cake flour
1 cup sugar
1 tbsp. baking powder
½ cup shortening
½ tsp. salt
½ cup milk
1 tsp. almond flavoring
4 egg whites

1. Sift the flour, measure, and sift again with the baking powder and salt. Set aside.

2. Cream together the sugar and shortening.

3. Add the flour mixture and the milk alternately to the

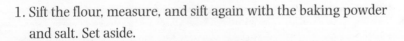

creamed sugar and shortening. Beat these ingredients thoroughly.

4. Stir in the almond flavoring.

5. Carefully mix in stiffly beaten egg whites.

6. Divide the batter into two 8" or 9" greased cake pans. Bake at 375°F for 20 minutes, or until done.

Fudge Icing

Ingredients

2 squares chocolate
1 tbsp. butter
2 cups sugar
Pinch of salt
⅔ cup milk
1 tsp. vanilla

1. Melt the chocolate squares.

2. Add sugar, milk, butter, and salt. Boil to soft ball stage (236°F).

3. Cool. Add vanilla and beat until creamy.

29

Every kid should grow a vegetable garden.

Most kids are long on enthusiasm, but short on patience. They'll expect sprouts to be popping through the ground the day after the seeds are planted, and after a week with no results, they may give up altogether. To keep them excited, their first gardening experience should happen quickly. Radishes make a perfect first veggie— hardy and quick-germinating, radishes are the perfect choice for the budding gardener.

Of course, not every child has acres of gardening space in the country. Even city dwellers can experience the wonder of plants— all you need is a small pot on a kitchen window. If you don't have a pot, you can give your child a coffee can (punch a few holes in the bottom with a hammer and nail for drainage), or cut the bottom from a large plastic jug—leave a few inches on the sides to hold in the dirt. Presto! Instant flower pot.

Here are some planting ideas that can work well in city gardens where space is limited.

Carrot Tops

The next time that you buy a bag of whole carrots, select one with a bit of green on the top. Slice off the top of the carrot and place it in a small bowl of water. Watch the top sprout!

Peas in a Pod

Give your child a few pea seeds to plant in a pot on a windowsill. Try the new sugar pea varieties—you can eat the pod and all. These germinate quickly and grow to a satisfying height.

Tomato Bush

Short on space? Try a tomato bush. That's right, tomato *bush*. There are several varieties of tomatoes that grow on bushes instead of vines. These potted bushes are small enough to fit just about anyplace; including a balcony, patio, or front porch. You can find them in gardening shops labeled "patio tomatoes."

For those with more space, here are some fun projects to try.

Zucchini-in-a-Bottle

Your child will be amazed when attempting to grow a zucchini in a bottle. Here's how to start:

1. Plant several zucchini seeds in the garden.

2. After the seeds have sprouted and grown into vines, they will flower, and then small zucchini will appear on the vines.

3. Once the small zucchini appear, carefully slip one into a clean, plastic, water or soda bottle. Since zucchini can grow to be large, you can grow them in several differently sized bottles.

4. Check on the bottled zucchini daily and cut them from the vine when they fill the bottles. Basically foolproof to grow, most any kind of squash should work for this project. Experiment to see which varieties work the best.

Sunny Sunflowers

While not technically a vegetable, sunflowers are the perfect complement to any vegetable garden. Averaging five to six feet (some grow above twelve feet), sunflowers are sure to be the hit of the garden!

Many varieties of sunflowers produce edible seeds that can be roasted for a great homegrown snack. If the variety you select is not edible, convince the kids to resist the urge to cut them down—they are *great* birdfeeders come fall.

Giant Vegetables

For those youngsters with access to a large garden, consider fruits and vegetables on a larger scale. Imagine the excitement at the

Labor Day picnic when you cut into the watermelon that your child grew in the backyard. Expecting a big turnout? Have no fear; some varieties grow to well over one hundred pounds!

Love Halloween? How about helping your child grow a three hundred–pound pumpkin? If you don't need something quite that big, try Baby Boo or Jack-Be-Little miniature pumpkins, or the white-skinned Lumina pumpkin, perfect for carving. Or experiment with one or more varieties of popcorn (grown on the cob), a favorite childhood snack.

30

Every kid should blow a bubble gum bubble until it pops.

People have been chewing gum ever since the ancient Greeks first popped some resin of the mastic tree into their mouths and started chomping away. The Mayan Indians in Central America chewed sap of the sapodilla tree called *chicle*, and Native Americans chewed spruce sap. Chewing gum was first commercially manufactured and sold in 1848 by John B. Curtis. He produced his spruce-based gum in a factory in Maine, but it didn't taste much like the sweet bubble gum we know—that was developed by twenty-three-year-old accountant Walter Diemer in 1928 at the Fleer Chewing Gum Company. Diemer, who came up with Dubble Bubble, added pink coloring to the first batch of his concoction (it was the only color he had available). The color proved to be so appealing that it was never changed.

However, you can pick any color you like when you and your kids make up a batch of the chewy confection in your own kitchen. Homemade bubble gum kits are available in many science and educational stores. If you *really* want to try making your own bubble gum from scratch, you'll find all you need (recipes, supplies, and kits) available online at www.leeners.com/gumrecipe.html.

Your homemade concoction might blow some pretty big bubbles, but it probably won't break the world's record. That distinction is held by Susan Montgomery Williams of Fresno, California, who produced a twenty-three-inch bubble on July 19, 1994 at the ABC-TV studios in New York.

While some folks like the gum, others like the package it comes in; the world's longest gum wrapper chain is currently 34,077 feet long (that's almost 6.5 miles) and it's being produced by Gary Duschl of Ontario, Canada. Gary began this record-setting chain on March 11, 1965, and so far he's used 792,691 wrappers.

With all this gum chewing going on, it's a cinch that sometime your child might get some stuck where it shouldn't be. While nothing is guaranteed, both peanut butter and ice cubes can be helpful in removing gum.

Rub a small amount of peanut butter into gum stuck in hair. Work it until the gum loosens and can be removed. For other items, like clothing and furniture, freeze the spot with an ice cube and then chip the gum away. Commercial removers are also available.

31

Every kid should experience a family car trip.

Ellen Moyer
Stay-at-home mom
Las Vegas, NV

With a little bit of preparation, you can turn car trip whines from, "Are we there yet?" to "Oh, man. We're there already?"

Let the kids navigate. Before the trip, get a map (or set of maps) for each child. Highlight the route you'll be taking, marking any major attractions you'll visit. Depending on how your trip is planned, consider highlighting each day's segment in a different color.

Be Prepared

Pack a "survival bag" for each child: in a paper lunch sack, pack several small toys, a drink box or two, and some relatively healthy snacks (crackers, cereal, nuts, granola bars, or dried fruit). Let your kids pick something out of their bag every one hundred miles, every hour, or when they need a new diversion. If you plan to travel in the car for several days, pack a separate bag for each day.

Sing!

No pop bands allowed. Turn off the radio and teach your children the songs you sang on car trips: "Row, Row, Row Your Boat" (in rounds, of course), "On Top of Spaghetti," "Old MacDonald (Had a Farm)," "B-I-N-G-O," and "She'll be Comin' 'Round the Mountain."

Play the A-B-C Game

"Collect" the letters of the alphabet in order from road signs, billboards, license plates, and other sources. First player to get to z wins. Before playing, decide among the players where the letters can come from. Also decide what to do about j, q, v, and other letters that might be difficult to find. This is a great game for younger children just learning their ABCs.

License Plate Spelling

This is a good game for older children. Make words with the letters in the license plates of passing cars. The letters must be used in the order they appear on the plate, but you don't need to use all of the letters. To score, give one point for each letter in the word, and an extra point for each letter from the license plate.

Two things to keep in the car for all car trips: a beach ball and a deck of cards. When you stop for a break, blow up the ball and let the kids play, then deflate it, pack it away, and you are ready to go. A deck of cards comes in handy for impromptu games of "Go Fish!" or "Old Maid"—perfect diversions if you are stuck in traffic or waiting for a table in a restaurant.

32

Every kid should see a classic movie on the big screen.

Thanks to cable TV, VCRs, and DVDs, children can enjoy the movies in the comfort of their own living room. Still, there's nothing quite like the big screen when it comes to something as scary as the flying monkeys from *The Wizard of Oz*, as majestic and beautiful as Disney's *Fantasia*, or as fun as singing along with the von Trapps while watching *The Sound of Music*. While your youngsters may have seen it a hundred times on video, there's something delightful about watching *Snow White & the Seven Dwarfs* at the theater. To add to the experience, check out classic movies like these at a revival movie house instead of a multi-screen cinema complex. And don't forget the popcorn—extra butter, please!

And then there's that very special experience of a drive-in movie. On a hot summer evening, every kid should go to a drive-in movie. Richard Hollingshead Jr. opened the first drive-in theater in 1933 in Camden, New Jersey, with room for five hundred cars. While all the rage in the 1950s, today there are fewer than a thousand drive-ins left. In fact, if you live in Alaska, Hawaii, Louisiana, or New Jersey, you won't find any drive-in theaters at all.

Finally, if the opportunity ever presents itself, every kid should see a 3-D movie in the theater. While these special films aren't produced very often these days, there's nothing like those in-your-face effects and cool, cardboard glasses.

And for sheer exhilaration, nothing beats an IMAX theater experience! You can find IMAX theaters at many planetariums and children's museums—but be aware that these special shows are really popular. They often sell out quickly, so if you plan to go, see if you can reserve your seats ahead of time. If you can't, go to the IMAX ticket counter first when you arrive at a museum and get your tickets early; then you can spend the time viewing the museum knowing that you've got your seats reserved.

MOVIES

33

Every kid should go to a parade.

From the first screams of the siren on the police car or fire truck leading the marchers to the last float, there are few things more thrilling than a parade when you are a kid. It doesn't matter if the parade is to welcome home the World Series champions, or just a small, hometown tradition to celebrate the Fourth of July. The air will be heavy with excitement and anticipation, and the street will be full of wonderful sites: marching bands parading together all in step; floats of all sizes, shapes, and colors; horses; cheerleaders; gymnasts; and clowns.

The best place to watch a parade is seated high atop Mom's or Dad's shoulders. If your child is too big for that, arrive early and grab a front-row, curbside seat. Remember to pack a blanket for the kids and maybe a lawn chair or two. And don't forget some bags so your child can bring home the loot collected during the parade.

While you're waiting for the parade to start, take in all the pre-parade sights and sounds, and enjoy a traditional parade-type snack: hot dogs, popcorn, cotton candy, or an ice cream cone. Once the parade begins, sit back and enjoy all the sights, sounds, and excitement that makes parades the spectacle they are.

If you're looking for something a little out of the ordinary, check out one of these parades:

- **The Bud Billiken Parade.** The second-largest parade in the U.S. is held each year in Chicago on the second Saturday in August.

- **The Chester Greenwood Day Parade.** Held each year on the first Saturday in December in Farmington, Maine, in honor of Chester Greenwood, the inventor of earmuffs.

- **The Do-Dah Parade.** A "salute to silliness" held each year on the first Saturday in June in Kalamazoo, Michigan.

- **The Fish House Parade.** This parade, featuring decorated ice shanties, is held each year on the Friday after Thanksgiving in Aitkin, Minnesota.

- **The Mother Goose Parade.** A celebration of favorite childhood rhymes and fairy tales, traditionally held the Sunday before Thanksgiving in El Cajon, California.

- **The Macy's Thanksgiving Day Parade.** The granddaddy of

them all is held each year on Thanksgiving morning in New York City.

For more information on these parades, or to find events in your area, check out the current edition of *Chase's Calendar of Events*. To find out what events are happening on "today's date," visit the Chase website at www.chases.com; click on "Today in Chase's" and find a list of all events happening worldwide. You can also find parade dates for large cities by searching the Internet for "New York City parades," "Chicago parades," and so on.

34

Every kid should write in a journal.

Jennifer Gralewski
College student
Riley Twp., MI

A place to write down hopes and dreams for the future, tales of adventures and explorations, or just doodle—every kid needs a journal. With some help from you, your child can craft a place to record childhood musings.

Start by deciding what size journal your child would like. Keep in mind that many papers are available in sheets as large as 12" x 12" giving your child a lot of options. After you've decided on the size, cut two pieces of cardboard (one for the front and one for the back), slightly larger than the size the pages will be. Cover the cardboard with paper, felt, fabric, or maybe even fake fur.

Thanks to the popularity of making scrapbooks and other crafts, you can find paper in every color, design, and pattern. Mix and match animal prints, plaids, polka dots, stripes, or whatever your child likes for the inside of the journal. Use a variety of decorative scissors to trim the top, bottom, and outside edge of the pages. Include decorative craft punches on the pages for an extra touch.

Punch several holes down one side on both the front and the back of the cover. Punch corresponding holes in each page of the scrapbook. To help the pages stay a part of the journal, add clear hole reinforcements to each page after it has been punched. Use binder rings to assemble the finished product. Add additional pages as needed.

Provide your child with an assortment of markers, pens, and pencils in a wide array of colors—now all that's needed is the inspiration!

What do you put in a journal? All sorts of things! Here are some ideas:

- **Friendship Journal.** Make a friendship journal and add craft ideas with instructions, drawings, poetry, short stories, pictures from magazines, cartoons, stickers, bookmarks, address labels, pressed flowers, and so on. Then wrap it up and give it to your friend!

- **Camping Journal.** Present your child with a journal to capture all the fun times during sleep-away camp. Have her include the daily schedule, her favorite sport, things she's learned. Let her new friends take turns writing in the journal. It will be a great souvenir in later years!

- **Dream Journal.** Have your child keep a journal by his bed. Each morning, he can jot down all that he can remember about last night's dreams.

- **Computer Journal.** If your child is computer savvy, let her keep a journal on a disk. Each night she can jot down thoughts about what she learned that day.

- **Alien Journal.** Let your child pretend he's on an alien mission to find out about earth. Each night, he can record something about earthlings that he's learned.

- **Self-awareness Journal.** Have your children think about who they are and what they stand for. What values are important to them?

- **Be Original.** The best journals are collections of feelings, thoughts, and ideas. Encourage your children to include favorite songs or poems, funny drawings, good jokes, and so on. Journals don't have to be simply pages and pages of full sentences and paragraphs.

35

Every kid should create a holiday keepsake.

Imagine the memories and emotions that will come rushing back when your children open a box full of Christmas ornaments that they have created throughout their childhood. There's that first ornament ever made, a small wooden star painstakingly painted yellow, the felt tree produced in third grade, the nativity meticulously crafted out of clay—a box full of memories your child can share someday with a future spouse and children.

The key to creating a box full of Christmas memories is to use materials that will hold up for twenty or thirty years—and more. Even the youngest kids can paint a wooden cutout or color a shrink plastic design. Or try craft foam, clay, fabric, plaster, and bread dough. For specific ornament ideas, check family-oriented or parenting magazines. Issues beginning in late fall often feature projects using a variety of supplies and techniques.

If your family celebrates other traditional holidays, help your child create an item in keeping with those traditions—a keepsake your family can enjoy now and your child's family can enjoy in the years to come. It's easier than you think to create a Hanukkah menorah or a Kinara for the celebration of Kwanzaa. All you'll need is:

Ingredients

1" x 4" piece of wood, 18–24" long
Wooden candle cups
Wooden blocks
Acrylic paints, in a variety of colors
Wood glue

1. Paint the wooden pieces using traditional or favorite colors and designs. Let dry.

2. Using wood glue, glue the wooden blocks, evenly spaced, to the 1" x 4" base. Use multiple blocks for more height, or to stagger the height of the candles.

3. Glue a candle cup on top of each block or stack of blocks.

Whatever your child makes, be sure there are a few extras. They make terrific keepsakes for grandparents, aunts, and uncles—and, of course, you're sure to want one, too.

36

Every kid should participate in a "-thon."

Most kids are generous; they're usually more than willing to pitch in and help raise money for a good cause. One fun way to raise money is to take part in some kind of "-thon." It doesn't matter if it's a read-a-thon, bike-a-thon, walk-a-thon, jump rope–a-thon, dance-a-thon, or rock-a-thon—what matters is that the proceeds go to a good cause.

After making the commitment to participate in the -thon, encourage your child to ask family, friends, and neighbors for sponsorship or donations. Depending on what the -thon is, your child may need some help preparing for it; take long walks to get ready for a walk-a-thon, or make sure the bike is in tip-top condition before a bike-a-thon. If it's a somewhat unusual -thon, check to find out what the world record for that particular activity is. It might be fun to see exactly how long, or how many times, someone did what your child is setting off to do.

For example, in 1930–31, one dance marathon lasted 5,154 hours and 48 minutes! Whatever the -thon is, remind your child that it doesn't matter how well he does, or how much money is raised—all that really matters is that he did something to help someone else and had a good time in the process.

If your child is saddened by a family whose house burned down or a school friend with an incurable disease, suggest that your child organize her own "-thon." Help her choose what she'd like to do, and then help gather together a group of friends to participate. To get ready for the -thon, your youngster will need to prepare some kind of form with information about the event so that the participants can collect pledges. Depending on the type of event, your child may need your help to find a -thon location, and to answer questions from other parents or potential donors. Unless you have a lot of adult support, try to keep the event and the number of participants small so that you and your child can handle it. It doesn't matter how much money the event generates, the recipient will be very grateful; not only for the money but for the time, energy, and heart that your child put into arranging it.

37

Every kid should possess a soft, cuddly stuffed animal, that he is never forced to give up because he's "too old."

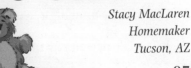

Stacy MacLaren
Homemaker
Tucson, AZ

Do you remember that worn, tattered bear with mismatched button eyes...packed away in a box or lost in a move, but who still holds a special place in your heart?

At some point during childhood, most children are attached to a stuffed animal of some sort; a special friend who keeps the bad dreams away, someone who listens to all their secrets, a constant companion. Imagine the devastation a child must feel when that beloved friend is lost in a fire, flood, tornado, or other natural disaster. Try to comprehend the heartbreak of leaving behind a best buddy.

Your child can help ease some of that heartache for another youngster, and make some space in the bedroom at the same time. Encourage your child to sort through all the stuffed animals and donate any that are in good shape—but that are no longer played with. Talk with your son or daughter about less fortunate children who don't have a special toy, and explain how happy that child would be to receive a beloved animal.

Once the animals are collected, give them a bath:

1. For best results, wash them inside pillowcases (you can pop several animals into one).

2. Fold the top over and secure with several large safety pins.

3. Wash the animals in a gentle cycle using a mild detergent.

4. Tumble dry on low until they are completely dry.

After the animals are clean, your child can help you reattach or replace loose or missing eyes, and add a brand-new ribbon around its neck. If your child enjoys refurbishing the stuffed animals, consider coordinating an animal drive in your neighborhood or with a local scout troop. After the animals are clean, the neighborhood kids or scout troop can work together to get the animals ready for their new homes.

When the animals are ready, donate them to local service agencies and shelters. Consider checking with local police and fire departments, who often keep a supply of stuffed animals for children in need. Wherever you decide to donate the animals, take your child along to see how much all that hard work means to someone else.

38

Every kid should have a collection.

Kids are natural collectors. But, what's the fun in collecting if the collection is stored in a shoebox on the top shelf of a closet where no one can enjoy it? Make collecting more exciting by helping your child display a collection in a fun and unique way. If your child has a valuable collection, take care to store and display it properly.

Encourage friends and family who travel for business or pleasure to send your child postcards from the places they visit. To make it easier, provide preprinted labels with your child's name and address. Frame the postcards and hang them in your child's room. They are easy to change as the collection grows.

If your friends or family travel abroad, ask them to bring back a few coins and paper currency for your child. Turn coins into pins by gluing on pin backs, or use them as charms for a necklace or bracelet by drilling a hole for the chain. Laminated paper currency make great bookmarks.

After opening the mail, give your child the empty envelopes for stamp removal. When the collection is big enough, help your child glue the stamps to a sheet of heavy paper or cardstock. Frame the stamp collage and hang it. Then start all over again.

Kids love to pick up rocks—big rocks, little rocks, shiny rocks, smooth river rocks, and really cool-shaped rocks. For very small rocks, attach heavy-duty magnets and decorate the refrigerator. Larger rocks can be displayed in a basket or empty fishbowl.

A button collection looks great when it's sewn onto a quilt and displayed on your child's bed. If that's a bit too ambitious for your child, suggest storing the collection in a large, old-fashioned jelly jar, or maybe a tin box, just like Great-Grandma probably did.

Most kids have stuffed animal collections. Display them in groups around your child's room, or if they're small enough, clip each one to a plastic chain suspended from the ceiling

Calling all conchologists! Your child can start a shell collection by picking up empty shells from the seashore, woods, parks, gardens, ponds, and streams. Garage sales can also be good places to look for shells! Your child can make a display box from a shoebox or shoebox lid, and label each shell with where it was found. Clean dirty shells with an old toothbrush and water; a bit of baby oil can make many shells shiny. Take your child to a museum or nature center that has a shell collection for ideas on how to display shells.

Model it! Whether it's dinosaurs, horses, dogs, or race cars, most kids have a passionate interest in something. Help them collect small china or plastic models of their heart's desire and build shelves or buy a bookcase to display the items.

39

Every kid should attend a live performance.

Going to the movies is a thrill for most children—the big screen, surround sound, and munchies. But there is something even more captivating about attending a live performance. Depending on what's available in your area and what interests your child, why not plan a trip to a concert, ballet, or the theatre?

If you plan to attend a concert, take some time before you go to introduce your child to different types of music and composers. If your collection isn't very big, borrow tapes or CDs from the library, or from family or friends. Play music during the day, through dinner and bath time, and while your child drifts off to sleep. An added benefit to all this music: research suggests that listening to music boosts math and thinking skills. If you don't have the opportunity to go to a symphony, check out a high school or college band or orchestra concert, or attend your town's local orchestra.

If you introduce your child to plays early in childhood, you may establish a lifelong love of theatre. Choose a children's production at a small, friendly community theatre for your first outing—the more interactive the better. If you're fortunate enough to live near a big city (especially New York) take your child on a special excursion to a child-friendly play at a professional theatre. If your child expresses a real interest in the theatre, check with your local community theatre for children's theatre classes during the summer— the perfect opportunity to give your young thespian a taste of the Great White Way.

For a very special treat, take your child to see a performance of the *Nutcracker Ballet* in December; it's performed by ballet companies in almost all large cities (and many smaller ones). Make this an event to underscore the importance and magic of the occasion—dress up in your finest, and consider going to tea at a fancy hotel afterwards. Before the show, give your child a *very* brief rundown of the story behind the ballet.

To make attending a live performance a positive experience for everyone, consider a matinee and try for a seat on the aisle, in case you have to leave early. Some very young children may only be able to sit through half a performance—that's OK! You're aiming to create some magic memories, not win a prize for endurance.

104

In many theatres, box seats for matinee performances are surprisingly reasonable. Consider splurging on box seats so that your little one can move around a bit more easily, and you can come and go (for drinks or bathroom breaks) without disturbing others. Your children will likely be fascinated with sitting in their own little "box"—it adds to the experience!

40

Every kid should let a fuzzy caterpillar crawl up her arm, and then watch that caterpillar turn into a butterfly.

Cheryl Cohen
Mom
Lancaster, PA

It doesn't matter what emerges from the cocoon; a stunning monarch butterfly or a plain, cabbage white butterfly; your child will delight in the anticipation of a new arrival.

Before your child ventures out on a caterpillar hunt, prepare a home for the new furry friend:

1. Cut out large sections of the side panels of a big shoebox, leaving a border 1" to 2" wide all the way around.

2. Duct tape window screen over the openings.

3. Cut a large section out of the lid and replace it with screen (It's important for the caterpillar to have as much ventilation and sunlight as possible).

Help your child place the caterpillar into its cage along with branches and leaves from the tree on which it was found. To help keep the sprigs fresh, wrap their ends with a moist cotton ball in aluminum foil. Help your child move the cage to a location where it won't be in direct sun during the day, and won't get too cold at night.

For more information on the caterpillar that your child is raising and what it will grow up to be, check out *Peterson First Guides to Caterpillars of North America* or *Young Naturalist Guide to Caterpillars*. If you don't have access to either of these books, continue to feed the caterpillar leaves from the tree on which it was found.

Collect rainwater to quench the caterpillar's thirst. Don't let your child put a container of water in the caterpillar's cage, as it may drown. Instead, your child can put a cotton ball moistened with rainwater in the bottom of the cage. Change the cotton ball when the leaves are changed. The caterpillar will also get moisture from the leaves.

While your child waits for the butterfly to be born, read *The Very Hungry Caterpillar* together.

Once the butterfly begins to flutter around its home, it's ready for its first flight. To increase the chances that your child's butterfly will stick around, and maybe even be joined by a few friends, plant some butterfly favorites in your yard—butterfly bush, daisies, delphinium, heliotrope, honeysuckle, hollyhock, lavender, milkweed, phlox, and even dandelions.

41

Every kid should create a self-portrait.

Do you remember that stick person with the goofy hair you proudly drew to represent yourself when you were five? What about the multidimensional person with actual facial features you drew when you were eight?

Here's a fun birthday tradition you may want to think about starting. Each year as your child's birthday approaches, hand out a piece of heavyweight, acid-free paper along with crayons, colored pencils, or markers. Instruct your child to draw a self-portrait—perhaps pictured with a friend, a favorite toy, or doing a favorite activity. Remember that whatever your child chooses to draw is OK.

When the portrait is complete, frame it and hang it beside the school pictures and other family portraits. Keep portraits from previous years right in the frame, or move them to a scrapbook, file cabinet, firebox, or other location where they can be safely stored.

Your child may also enjoy creating a life-sized self-portrait. To create this, tape a large piece of white paper to the floor. Have your child lie down in the middle of the paper, and trace around your child's body. Then your child can color in hair, facial features, and a favorite outfit.

You can also create a permanent life-sized portrait:

1. Trace your child's outline on a piece of plywood.

2. Carefully cut it out using a jigsaw or coping saw.

3. Sand any rough edges.

4. Cover the cutout (front and back) with a coat of white latex primer, and let dry completely.

5. Use acrylic craft paint to add skin tone and facial features.

6. Paint on the hair (or glue on yarn or commercial doll hair).

7. Decide how the wooden cutout should be dressed. Your child can paint a fun outfit or undergarments—and then dress the cutout in actual children's clothes.

Stood in a bedroom, the cutout is a great place to hang your child's favorite ball cap or jacket.

42

Every kid should build a sand castle in the summer and a snow fort in the winter.

Because the techniques for building fabulous snow forts and super sand castles are virtually the same, you and your kids will have twice as many opportunities to master the techniques. The basis for building a terrific sandcastle or snow fort is to start with the right materials. For best results, use wet sand, or good packing snow.

For the actual construction, a number of things found right around the house can be used to mold a variety of shapes:

- Milk cartons: staple the top closed and cut off the bottom to create watchtowers. Or, cut off the top and use the bottom for towers, or cut into smaller sections for bricks.

- Loaf pans—regular and mini: great for basic building bricks.

- Two-liter plastic soda pop bottles: cut the top section off. Use the bottom for towers and pillars. Fill the top section to create unusual tower toppers.

- Plastic spoons and knives: handy for scooping out sections and cutting pieces down in size.

- Also see what your child can do with bundt pans, gelatin molds, funnels, plastic butter tubs, muffin tins, and a variety of shapes and sizes of plastic food-storage containers.

If your child finds that the snow or sand is sticking in the molds, spray the inside of the mold with a light coat of non-stick cooking spray before packing the snow or sand into it. Add color to your snow fort by "spray painting" it with a mixture of *cold* water and food coloring in a squirt bottle.

Create unique accessories for the snow fort by freezing plain or colored water in a variety of containers. If your child has difficulty removing the ice shapes, you can dip the mold in warm water for a minute or two until the ice releases from the mold. Challenge your child to create an entire structure from the ice shapes.

Finish up a long day of sand-castle construction with a nice, cold snow cone. And there is nothing nicer than a mug of hot cocoa with lots of marshmallows after an afternoon spent building a snow fort!

43

Every kid should go on a factory tour.

Becky Ballance
Elementary school teacher
Goodrich, MI

"How do they make..." As a parent, you've probably been asked that question a thousand times. Instead of trying to explain, you can show your child how a favorite snack or toy is made—by going on a factory tour! Many factories and companies offer tours of their facilities. Check with tour and guide books for tours in your area or vacation destination.

Before planning a factory tour as part of your vacation, call ahead for details. Be sure to check tour availability, days and time of operation, cost, age requirements or restrictions, and accessibility. It is also a good idea to get directions to the factory. If possible, make reservations or schedule a tour for a specific date and time. For families who can't travel to take an actual factory tour, many companies offer "virtual tours" via the Internet.

For a real tour on a somewhat smaller scale, you don't need to look much further than your own backyard. You'll often find that local TV or radio stations, bakeries, restaurants, fire or police departments, hospitals, and other businesses are more than happy to give you and your kids a personal tour. Call around and see what you can arrange.

Here's a brief roundup of some fun famous places to try.

Color It Fun!

A whole world of creativity awaits your child in every brand-new box of crayons. You and your child can see how markers are produced and how crayons are made, labeled, and packaged at The Crayola Factory, an interactive discovery center, at Two Rivers Landing in Easton, Pennsylvania—and get some free samples to take home, too.

Summer Fun!

Summer just wouldn't be summer without ice cream and baseball. If travel plans permit, you can watch baseball bats being turned at the Louisville Slugger factory in Louisville, Kentucky. With samples included in the tour, the Ben & Jerry's ice cream factory tour in Waterbury, Vermont, is the perfect stop on a hot summer day.

Kellogg's

Start your day off right with a good breakfast and a trip to Kellogg's Cereal City USA in Battle Creek, Michigan. Kellogg's Cereal City USA features a reproduction cereal production line where you can watch Kellogg's Corn Flakes being made, just like they are in the actual factory.

Hug a Bear

Almost every child has owned a teddy bear. Kids (and moms and dads, too) can watch teddy bears being made in San Francisco, California, at The Basic Brown Bear Factory, America's oldest real working teddy bear factory.

Snack Foods

Potato chips, cheese curls, tortilla chips, or pretzels—whatever your family favorite, you can watch them all being made with a tour of Herr's Snack Factory in Nottingham, Pennsylvania. While you're in the area, you can visit the original Sturgis pretzel museum and factory in Lititz, Pennsylvania, about an hour from Nottingham. Also at Lititz you'll find the Wilbur Chocolate Factory (home of the famous Wilbur Buds)—and just a short forty-five-minute hop is another factory tour—Hershey Chocolates in Hershey, Pennsylvania.

Jelly Belly Beans

If you're in the Fairfield, California, area, stop in and watch Jelly Belly jelly beans being produced in an actual candy factory. Pick up a free sample after your tour.

44

Every kid should decorate the driveway.

Your driveway is a huge, empty canvas for your child, perfect for drawing life-sized renderings of family and friends, enormous tic-tac-toe games, and giant doodles. They'll have a great time drawing colossal daisies to celebrate spring...balloons to celebrate a birthday...a bigger-than-life worksheet for practicing multiplication tables, spelling words, or writing a poem.

The next time the rain is busy cleaning off the most recent driveway masterpiece, help your child to make up a batch of sidewalk chalk to use on the next sunny day.

Make-Your-Own Sidewalk Chalk

Ingredients
Newspaper
Waxed paper
Masking tape
1 cup plaster of paris
Clear or white liquid dish soap
Liquid tempera paint, in a variety of colors
10-oz. plastic cups, one for each piece of colored chalk you make
Toilet paper tubes, one for each piece of chalk you make
Craft sticks or disposable plastic spoons, one for each piece of
chalk you make

1. Cover the work area with newspaper.

2. Tape a piece of waxed paper tightly around the bottom
   of the tube.

3. Measure and pour plaster of paris into a plastic cup.

4. Add ⅓ cup + 1 tablespoon cool water, and a few drops of
   dish soap. Stir until the plaster is completely dissolved.

5. Mix in liquid tempera paint to the desired color (one to
   three tablespoons). Note: the color will darken as it dries.

6. Stir until the mixture thickens slightly.

7. Spoon or pour the mixture into the tube, filling it almost to the top.

8. Set on a warm plate and move to a warm, dry location.

9. When the chalk is dry, tear the tube away from the chalk.

10. Repeat with a different color of paint for as many pieces of chalk as you wish to make.

45

Every kid should write a "memory letter" each year.

When your child is all grown up, how much will he or she remember of childhood? Will your daughter remember kicking the winning goal in the only game her soccer team won that year? Will your son remember the theme of his birthday party, and who came? What about the favorite toys, books, TV shows, musical group, song—even best friend?

Spend the week before New Year's Day helping your child chronicle the year that is ending by writing a letter to be opened at a predetermined date in the future. With your help, your child will be able to save all those memories.

Before beginning, talk to your child about the best way to remember all the major events for the past year. Perhaps your child

121

may choose to work on the letter chronologically, looking at what happened month-by-month. Perhaps a topical or random look at thoughts and memories will make more sense. To help your child remember all the things that have happened over the twelve months, keep a file during the year with notes, random thoughts, and newspaper clippings. The family calendar is also a great tool for jogging the memory.

Consider writing a letter for your child who is too young to write a letter unassisted. Include a list of favorite things along with information about the activities of the past year. Be sure to include several of your child's thoughts or quotes, transcribed verbatim.

When the letter is finished, add photographs, newspaper clippings, school papers, artwork, and maybe a copy of the family calendar from the year. Mom or Dad might even want to slip in a note. Put the letter, along with any miscellaneous items, in a large envelope. Label the envelope with your child's name and: "Do Not Open until New Year's Day ____." Fill in the blank with the year your child will be eighteen, twenty-one, twenty-five, or whatever year you and your child determine the letters should be opened. Store it away in a safe place, with the letters from previous years.

46

Every kid should explore other cultures.

Sharon Naylor
Author
East Hanover, NJ

*Brazil...Germany...China...Spain...Norway...Mexico...Thailand...
Kenya...Australia...Peru...Greenland...Iceland...Ghana...Sweden...
Austria...Ireland...Italy...Poland...Portugal...Japan...Venezuela...
Zimbabwe...France...India...Guatemala...New Zealand...Russia...*

There are a world of places the typical child may never visit—
but that doesn't mean they can't be experienced.

Select a place that interests you and your child, or where you
would like to visit. Use the library, travel or visitor bureaus, and

travel agencies to collect information about the country. If your children are computer literate, help them find information about the country of your choice using a search engine (two popular choices: www.google.com or www.metacrawler.com)

Find out things like: where is it? Are there mountains, plains, lakes, or volcanoes? What's the weather like? What unusual animals live there? What are the people like? What language do they speak? What do they wear? What do they eat? What kinds of houses do they live in? What holidays do they celebrate? What do they do for fun? Get a map of the country, and as many brochures with color pictures as possible. If possible, get a video featuring the people of the country, or even a video of the country itself.

Younger children might be satisfied with an afternoon's worth of information, but older children may be interested enough to spend as much as a week or more learning about the country.

Working with your child, start out by planning a trip to the country. Determine how you will get there, how long it will take, and how much it might cost. Make a list of specific cities and attractions you'd like to see while you are there.

Figure out how you will communicate while you are there. Even with audio or video tapes, there are some foreign languages that are very difficult to learn. Pick out some words that you might need: "hotel," "restaurant," "market," "hospital," and "police." Learn to recognize these words when you see them.

If you are able to locate the correct ingredients, or reasonable substitutes, spend a day in the kitchen with your child preparing a traditional meal of that country.

After you've taken an in-depth look at several different cultures, suggest that your child imagine what a trip to Venus might be like. What are the people like? What language do they speak? What are the must-see attractions and other hot spots? Celebrate a Venusian holiday, complete with traditional Venusian foods. Create a passport for your child, and document all the places that you "visit."

47

Every kid should play dress-up.

There's nothing like pretending to be a knight in shining armor, slaying a dragon...or a firefighter, rescuing a kitty from a tree...or a fairy princess, living in a castle surrounded by a moat full of alligators...or a silly circus clown...or even Mom or Dad. Playing dress-up is the perfect way to spend a rainy afternoon stuck indoors. Imagine the possibilities!

Clearance sales after Halloween are a great time to buy costumes and accessories at very reasonable prices. In a large box, collect:

- Old purses

- Scarves

- Jewelry

- Ties

- Gowns

- Shoes (sandals and high heels)

- Shirts

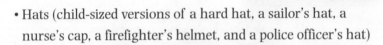

- Hats (child-sized versions of a hard hat, a sailor's hat, a nurse's cap, a firefighter's helmet, and a police officer's hat)

It doesn't really matter exactly what's in the box; your child can turn something in the box into exactly what's needed. With a little help from you, your child can create whatever accessories are lacking from the dress-up box. For example:

- Armor: with a large piece of heavy cardboard and some aluminum foil, the two of you can create a set of armor, complete with sword.

- Masks: with a piece of craft foam or thin cardboard, you can help your child create an array of masks for the box. Cut the foam or cardboard into a full-face or Mardi Gras–style mask. Punch a hole in each side of the mask and attach a piece of thin elastic. Your child can turn the mask into anything—a lion, a tiger, a bear, a dog, or even a favorite animated character.

- Doctor/nurse: make a face mask with a square of white sheet and four cotton strings. Add a doctor kit and a white coat.

• King/Queen: draw the outline of a crown on a piece of medium-thickness cardboard. Let your child decorate it with paints and fake "jewels"; then bend the crown and staple the ends together. Add a long piece of rich material as the "royal robes."

48

Every kid should eat green eggs.

What better way to turn a child on to reading than by bringing some favorite books and literary characters to life? Why not make a pot of *Stone Soup* for dinner, or see how many small beanbag animals will fit inside *The Mitten*? How about turning your child's room into a place *Where the Wild Things Are* or prepare a batch of muffins fit for a moose? Be careful, you know what happens *If You Give a Moose a Muffin*.

For Dr. Seuss fans of all ages, why not commemorate the date of his birth (March 2, 1904) with a batch of green eggs? But beware, these treats are not quite what they seem. You may like them so much that you'll eat them with a fox, in a box, in the rain, on a train, here and there and *anywhere*. Snack on the green eggs while you read *Green Eggs and Ham* with your child. Here's how:

1. Put two cups of white chocolate or vanilla chips into a

heavy-duty zipper bag. Seal the bag and put it into a large bowl of hot tap water. Replace the water as needed until the chips are melted.

2. Remove the bag from the water and knead gently to break up any small, unmelted pieces.

3. Snip off a *small* corner of the bag, and squeeze half-dollar-sized blobs of chocolate onto a cookie sheet covered with waxed or parchment paper.

4. Tap the cookie sheet on the counter to smooth out the tops of the eggs.

5. Place one green M&M candy ("m" side down) in the middle of each blob. The chocolate starts to harden quickly, so work fast!

6. Let harden. Store in an airtight container. Makes about three dozen eggs, depending on size.

Note: if the chocolate starts to harden in the bag, place it back in the water, cut corner up, and remelt the chocolate.

49

Every kid should ride a horse.

Norma Testa
Executive Director
Wilmington, DE

At some point during childhood, almost every child wants a horse. Some even go as far as devising a whole plan to feed, brush, and care for the horse every day after school, and stake out a corner in the backyard for the barn they've designed. Sadly, owning a horse isn't a realistic option for most children. But that doesn't mean that they can't experience the fun of riding one.

Look for a local stable that offers riding lessons or trail riding. Unless your child is an experienced rider, you'll need to find a stable that offers proper training before letting you ride alone. You'll also need safety equipment—at the very least, a hard riding hat. Some stables require shoes with a heel as well—no sneakers! Check with the stable to see what items they have that you can rent or borrow. Until you decide that riding is something your child enjoys and wants to continue, there's no need to invest in expensive riding equipment.

If the whole horseback-riding experience makes your child want a horse even more, see if you and your child can stay after your ride to observe or maybe even help with the chores. There's always work around a barn! If the thought of all that work doesn't deter your child, explain that keeping a horse in your backyard (even if you had the space for one) isn't an option—but your child can still ride occasionally.

On the evenings that your child doesn't get to enjoy a horse ride, why not enjoy a horse story together? Read a chapter or two aloud from *National Velvet*, *Black Beauty*, *My Friend Flicka*, *White Fang*, or *Misty of Chincoteague*.

50

Every kid should have a treasure box.

Silver half-dollars left by the tooth fairy...The shell of a robin's egg found on a walk through the woods...A Valentine's Day card from a third grade crush... A really neat cat's eye marble, found in the dirt at the playground...A dried starfish discovered at the beach last summer...

Half the fun of collecting treasures is having a really cool place to keep them safe from nosey little brothers and sisters. Here's how your child can create a personal treasure box to stash away priceless childhood mementos:

1. Choose the box—perhaps a cardboard pencil box or a shoebox.

2. Select a paper to cover the box—wrapping paper, tissue paper, craft or scrapbook paper, or old maps all work well.

3. Tear the paper into small pieces, 2" to 3" square.

4. Dip them into a mixture of two parts white craft glue and one part water.

5. Cover the box (depending on the paper, it may take more than one layer for complete coverage).

6. After the box is dry, use dimensional craft paint (available in many colors, including glitter and glow-in-the-dark) to add more decorations to the box, inside and out.

51

Every kid should spend some time on a farm, even for a short visit.

Michele Pacholka
Elementary school teacher
Sanford, MI

Unless they live on a farm or have family who does, most children don't know much about the agricultural way of life.

They *know* that milk comes from cows, eggs come from chickens, and wool comes from sheep, but they don't make that connection when they are drinking that glass of milk, eating that omelet, or wearing that sweater. And while they do realize that someone grew all those fruits and vegetables in the produce department of the grocery store, they have no idea what it takes to produce food on that kind of scale. Even though they've seen it on TV and read about it in stories, many children don't really believe that a rooster sounds the wake-up call each morning on the farm.

If your child isn't quite sure how the milk gets from the cow to the grocery store, it's time to spend an afternoon visiting an "educational farm." Educational farms are usually working farms on a much smaller scale, with a few cows, sheep, goats, chickens, pigs, or other livestock along with some small fields. Depending on the farm that you visit, your child may get to feed the animals, milk a cow, collect eggs from the chicken coop, and maybe try spinning wool into yarn after helping to shear a sheep.

If you can't find an educational farm, contact working farms in your area to see if you can arrange a visit for you and your child. An educational farm will give your child a more hands-on experience, but a trip to a working farm will show how things are really done. For example, your child may not realize that cows are no longer milked by hand. Regardless of the type of farm you visit, reinforce what your child has learned by talking about the farm products you see at the grocery store and use at home.

If you're the adventurous sort, you can also arrange to spend a holiday on a working farm. You can find working farms that take paying guests in all parts of the country, and it's the perfect way to combine a relaxing getaway with a real educational experience for your child! Most of these bed-and-breakfast farms allow children to help out finding eggs, milking cows, or taking a pony ride. To find a list of farm vacations, try the Pennsylvania Farm Vacation Association, a group that checks out the farms and maintains a website describing each of the farms at: www.pafarmstay.com (or call (888)856-6622.) You can also find a list of vacation farms at Vermont Farm Vacations, www.vermontfarms.org/farmvac.htm. If you'd prefer a farm vacation in another part of the country, simply use a search engine (such as www.google.com) for "farm vacations."

52

Every kid should be allowed the freedom to make choices, decisions, and mistakes.

For a parent, it's second nature to shelter and protect your child from anything that might cause injury, pain, heartache, or upset. You make the best possible choices to help your child avoid situations that may arise as a result of the decisions that are made. After

138

all, you have had many more years of life experiences; you have already made the mistakes and learned from them. But you learned *because* you made the mistakes and dealt with the fallout.

Children can start to make decisions for themselves from a very young age. If you will be running errands for the morning, let your child select a pair of pants and a shirt to wear. Don't be too embarrassed by the striped pants and polka-dot shirt your child insisted on wearing; any parent who has ever had small children will understand. You can also help your child practice making decisions by offering two or three choices from which to select. For example, for lunch, you might let your child choose between a peanut butter and jelly sandwich or a bowl of macaroni and cheese.

While you're helping your young child learn to make decisions, also teach that some decisions have negative consequences. For example, making the decision to leave toys lying around the family room may result in those toys being taken away for a period of time. Or deciding to play outside rather than do homework might result in an after-school detention, which would mean no baseball practice that day.

Allow more decisions and choices as your child gets older. Unless the choice or decision is illegal or could lead to serious injury, let your child deal with any negative outcomes as a result of the decision. As hard as it may be for your child to believe when it happens, no one ever died because the purple hair dye didn't wash out like promised on the package.

If you feel that your child isn't ready to make decisions completely alone, talk about the choices and the possible results of each of those choices. Reinforce the values and beliefs you have shared and trust your child to make the best decision.

53

Every kid should go to a fair, carnival, or amusement park.

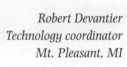

Robert Devantier
Technology coordinator
Mt. Pleasant, MI

No place on earth captures the essence of childhood quite like a fair, carnival, or amusement park. There's something about the sights, sounds, smells, and tastes that epitomize all the best of being a child. Stuffing yourself full of cotton candy, elephant ears, french fries, and lemonade...riding the roller coaster until you feel sick—and then riding nine more times. Spending three weeks worth of allowance to win a small stuffed bear. Just being a kid, without a care in the world.

All across America, the highlight of the summer is the county fair. Many kids (and some adults) spend months preparing projects. They raise animals; grow vegetables; put up jam, jelly, or preserves; or complete a needlework project. No trip to the fair is complete without a walk through the exhibition hall. Perhaps your child will be inspired to enter a project.

Many towns have an annual fair, festival, or carnival to celebrate the town's heritage, or the primary local crop or industry—blueberries, maple syrup, or cereal, for example. These events offer the entire town an opportunity to get together and promote the best features of the town. They offer parents and children the opportunity to spend a few hours together simply having fun, so take the time to take your child to that fair, and be a kid again yourself.

To find a fair, check out the U.S. State and County Fairs website at www.expocentral.com/agriculture/us_fairs/US_Fairs.html. Links for fairs in each state are listed, ranging from California (thirty-eight fairs) and Pennsylvania (twenty) to West Virginia and Utah (one each).

54

Every kid should visit the place(s) where Mom and Dad grew up.

All you have to do is start a sentence with, "When I was your age..." and eyes will start to roll. Your child probably knows all those stories by heart!

Because of job transfers and other relocations, you may not live in the same town where you were raised. Has your child ever visited the places where you *really* grew up? The places where your childhood memories were made?

Schedule a trip to the elementary school you attended. Walk the halls where your artwork was displayed and where you and your best friend exchanged notes between classes...the hall that seemed a mile long that time you were sent to the principal's office.

Pull out your old school sweatshirt or varsity jacket and go to a sporting event at your former middle school or high school. Celebrate, regardless of the outcome, with a pizza at the same pizzeria where you celebrated wins and mourned losses with your friends.

Hike into the woods near the house you grew up in. Find the majestic maple tree in whose branches you whiled away the long, lazy days of summer—the same tree you spent hours propped against, lost in a book, and whose leaves you pressed between the pages of those books.

Stop for an ice cream at the little stand where your Dad took you after baseball practice on hot summer afternoons to sneak a cone before dinner. Mom never let on that she knew.

Visit the corner store where you went with your friends. A monumental landmark, it was the first place your Mom let you go alone—where you spent your allowance on bubble gum, trading cards, soda pop, and other really neat stuff.

Share these places with your child, and you may be surprised at the impact it has.

55

Every kid should get dressed up and go to a fancy dinner or restaurant.

For most children, the only opportunity they have to get dressed for a fancy meal is an occasional wedding or other special family affair. As a result, they may have no idea what to do when faced with all that silverware, and their table manners may not be quite what they should be. Turn the task of brushing up on table manners into a fun experience for the whole family.

After a trip to the library for a few resources on how to set a table and basic manners, give your child a large piece of paper for each member of the family. Have your child draw a complete table setting, including a complete array of silverware, plates, and bowls. Using everyday dinnerware or even paper plates and plastic silverware, practice setting and eating with complete table settings. After several successful meals, it's time to break out the fine linen, silver, china, and crystal.

With your fine china and crystal at stake, you might prefer to set the table yourself. Keep your child involved and entertained by assigning the task of folding the napkins into decorative shapes. Pick up a few books on napkin folding while you're at the library. Depending on the directions, you may need to do some interpreting or instructing. Challenge your child to try folding a bishop's mitre, a maid's cap, an envelope, or maybe even a rosebud tucked into an empty water goblet. Encourage your child to fold a special creation for each member of the family. After the napkin creations are complete, your child can practice penmanship while creating special place cards for everyone.

After everyone has mastered the art of using a complete table setting correctly and polished up their table manners, reward the family with an opportunity to get all dressed up and venture out to a restaurant to show off what they have learned.

56

Every kid should create a board game.

Carol Turkington
Writer
Mohnton, PA

Almost all kids love to play games—and what could be more fun than designing your own! The first step is to come up with a theme—will you create a spaceship game? Will it be based on a favorite literary or cartoon character? If your child is stumped for an idea, suggest a favorite movie, hobby, or sport. Brainstorm with your child and see what the two of you can come up with. Then help your child make a general plan for the game, including layout, rules, game pieces, game cards, and so on. Now, you're ready to begin!

The Board

The first step is to find the board. Check garage sales or thrift shops for an old board game, or recycle a game you no longer play with. For a unique game board, cut a piece of foam-core board or heavy cardboard. Cut a piece of heavy-bond paper or lightweight cardboard the same size as the game board. In case of design changes or mistakes, don't affix the paper or cardboard to the game board until it's completed. Or you can use a roll of wrapping paper to cover the board (many printed gift wraps are white on the reverse side).

Spinners/Dice

Depending on the rules your child has decided on for the game, you may need a traditional spinner or dice borrowed from another game—or use small wooden blocks to create custom dice. Educational stores also carry commercial "blank" dice your child can customize.

Game Pieces

Your child may borrow game pieces from other games, or use small items from around the house, such as buttons, bottle caps, beads, pasta noodles, coins, or maybe rocks. You can create game pieces out of clay. Crayola Model Magic is an easily moldable material that hardens when air-dried.

Box

When the game is finished, cover the lid of the box from the game you recycled with white paper so that your child can decorate a box to store the game and all of its pieces.

If your child prefers puzzles to board games, help your child create one by using markers to draw a picture on the back of an assembled, store-bought puzzle. Voila! Instant personal puzzle.

57

Every kid should have one outstanding teacher.

Do you remember the teacher who made an indelible impression on you and had a profound impact on your future? The teacher who was willing to climb up onto the desk to make a point. The teacher who dressed up like Abraham Lincoln and delivered the Gettysburg Address from memory. The teacher who made science fun by lighting a bulb with a potato battery.

If your child isn't fortunate enough to have a teacher like that, *you* can be the one to provide those experiences:

- Create a word-search puzzle from spelling or vocabulary words. Or try your hand at creating clues and an accompanying crossword puzzle with the words.

- Reinforce fractions by baking half a batch of chocolate chip or oatmeal raisin cookies. Or better yet, double the recipe!

- Bring the lessons of government class to life with a trip to the state capital.

- Stage an archaeological dig in the backyard. Bury several plastic dinosaurs in the sandbox, and provide your child with clues to discover their location. After the dig, spend an afternoon exploring dinosaur remains at a local museum.

- Use a package of multicolored candies to practice percentages or to create bar graphs. Eat the results.

- Get the real story. Many large libraries have large newspaper and magazine archives. When your child is studying an event that occurred within the last one hundred years, go to the library to look up firsthand accounts of the event. What did people say when the Titanic sank...when the Hindenberg exploded...during World War II? Use advertisements and other articles in the newspapers and magazines to build a more complete picture of life during that time. Look up headlines from the day your child was born.

58

Every kid should write a letter to a favorite actor, athlete, or hero.

Most kids have a celebrity they respect and admire. Maybe it's a TV actor, a favorite author, or a member of their top sports team. Maybe it's an astronaut, explorer, or someone who has done something really cool.

But while most people can recite the accomplishments of a favorite hero, most of us have probably never thought about taking the time to send a fan letter. Why not suggest that your child write a letter to a favorite celebrity—to ask a question or two, request an autograph or photograph, or just to share some thoughts. Here are a few pointers to help your child:

- Make the letter readable. If possible, type it up on a computer.

- Keep the letter short. The celebrity to whom your child is writing probably receives a lot of mail.

- Enclose a self-addressed, stamped envelope. Not only can answering fan mail be very expensive, but what if the letter with your child's name and address gets misplaced? Your child has a better chance of getting a reply if there's an SASE.

- Once the letter is finished, take a trip to the library to check a reference book of celebrity addresses. The librarian should be able to help you and your child find what you need.

- Occasionally, letters come back as undeliverable. Explain to your child that just like "regular" people, celebrities move or change their post office boxes. Try to find a more current address. Also explain to your child that there may be no reply for a long time. Remind your child that the celebrity is very busy.

Encourage your child to write other letters. Instead of complaining to you, suggest that your child write to the president of the cereal company voicing dissatisfaction about the lack of marshmallows in the "new and improved formula." Show your child how to use the power of words to express passionate opinions.

153

59

Every kid should have a pet.

Carmen Wlezien
Sales manager
Plainfield, IL

What child hasn't begged Mom or Dad for a pet? But as any parent who has ever had one knows, a pet comes with a lot or responsibility and hard work.

If your child has been pestering you for a pet, you can try an animal on a short-term basis. Many classrooms have a small caged "pet" in the room—usually a gerbil, hamster, or guinea pig. Volunteer your child to take care of the class pet during the summer. If your child is unable to accept the responsibility, *you* only have to take care of it for a few months, at most.

If you decide that your child (and the rest of the family) is ready for a pet, spend some time researching the perfect animal for your situation. For example, if no one is at home during the day, a puppy might not be the best choice for your family. Talk to owners and breeders and read articles on types of pets. The more information that you collect, the better decision you can make. After all, this new family member could be with you for the next ten to twenty years. Don't forget to stop by the local animal shelter. Shelters often have beautiful, purebred animals looking for new homes because their owners relocated or another family member was allergic to it.

If you're looking for a particular breed, ask your vet if there is a "rescue breed organization" in your area. These groups specialize in one breed—golden retrievers, beagles, or greyhounds, for example—and will have many purebred animals that have been abandoned or given to the rescue group to find a new home.

Even if a pet isn't an option for your family because of your living arrangements or health concerns, your child can still gain some of the benefits that come from having a pet. Let your child volunteer to walk the dog for the elderly woman across the street every day after school (this will be especially appreciated on rainy and snowy days). Contact your local animal shelter and ask what your child can do there to help.

If your child's allergies prevent you from having a pet, check with your child's doctor for types of animals or treatment options that might make a pet possible for your family.

While pets might mean extra responsibilities and expenses for the entire family, the lessons of unconditional love and companionship they teach last a lifetime.

Z ^Z z

60

Every kid should have a hobby.

Every parent has heard it at one time or another: "I'm bored. There's nothing to do." If you've heard it more than your fair share of times, maybe it's time to find your child a hobby.

When choosing a hobby, it's important to be realistic. Your child may love horses, but taking up horseback riding may not be the best choice if you live in an apartment in a major metropolitan area. It's also important to choose something in which your child appears to be genuinely interested. If your child has shown an interest in your hobby, this might be the perfect opportunity to share it.

If your child isn't interested in your hobby, try to find something that you both think might be fun. Don't immediately discount a potential hobby because you don't know much about it or because you don't know anyone who knows much about it. Put the word out among your friends and coworkers. Someone is bound to know someone who can help you out. Also consider locating an organization or guild with members who specialize in the hobby your child has chosen.

Once your child has selected a hobby and you have found an expert to help out, learn as much as you can about the hobby yourself. This will not only help you discuss the hobby intelligently with your child, but you'll be able to make informed decisions when you buy supplies. Remind your child that mastering any new skill takes hard work, determination, patience, and time.

There are all kinds of hobbies out there—here's a list to get you started:

- Ceramics

- Pottery

- Knitting

- Sewing

- Stained glass

- Harmonica playing

- Photography

- Race cars

- Watercolors

- Archery

- Biking

- Swimming

- Model building

- Stamp collecting

- Creating cardboard villages

- Airplane models

- Model railroading

- Model shipbuilding

- Juggling

- Kite flying

- Puppetry

- Magic

- Soapmaking or candlemaking

61

Every kid should decorate her room according to the theme of her choice.

Most kids spend more than a third of their childhood sleeping, studying, and playing in their bedroom. So shouldn't you help your child turn that room into the perfect place? While some compromise might be required, you can make over your child's room with little more than a couple of gallons of paint and a few yards of fabric.

- If your child is going through a tiger phase, why not paint the room orange with black stripes?

- Create red walls with black spots during a ladybug stage.

- Painting all four walls in a small room might be too much, but painting one wall might be just enough to set the tone for the room. There are wall paints on the market today that guarantee one-coat coverage over *any* color, as long as the surface is properly prepared and all other manufacturer's directions are followed.

- Fabric is available in every color and pattern imaginable. With a few yards of fabric in a color or pattern to match or complement the theme, you can sew up simple panel curtains and update an old comforter with a duvet cover.

- Buy filmy fabric and drape it over your daughter's four-poster or canopy bed. Or attach a curtain rod above the bed along the wall and ceiling and drape the fabric over the rods.

- Create one-of-a-kind, decorator sheets with fabric craft paints and dyes.

- Paint an unfinished dresser, nightstand, or bookcase with leftover wall paints.

- Use acrylic craft paints to craft custom floor coverings and window shades by painting theme-related designs on canvas throw rugs and plain window shades.

- Cut simple, thematic shapes out of wood for wall decorations, shelves, or bookends.

- For a sixties look, hang beads in the doorway, add a lava lamp, some "flower power" rugs, and tie-dye sheets and pillowcases.

- For an African safari, drape mosquito netting from your son's bunkbed, and add some large stuffed wild things—lions, tigers, bears.

62

Every kid should take a trip to Washington, D.C.

Lou Ballance
Handyman
Goodrich, MI

During his presidency, George Washington selected the site that is now Washington, D.C., to be the capital of the United States. He hired Pierre Charles L'Enfant, a French architect and engineer, to design the new city. A residence for the president, not officially named the White House until 1901, was begun in 1792. In 1800, the capital of the United States was moved from Philadelphia to Washington, D.C.

While there is more to do and see than you can possibly take in during a single trip, there are a number of kid-friendly attractions that are worth seeing. As time permits, consider visiting:

- **The White House.** Located at 1600 Pennsylvania Avenue, the White House has been home to every president except George Washington. When the exterior of the White House starts to look dingy, it takes 570 gallons of paint to give it a fresh look.

- **Washington Monument.** This monument to the nation's founding father towers above the city. There are now 896 steps from the base to the top (two have been removed over the years). The original steam-powered elevator was replaced by an electric one in 1901, shortening the ride to the top from twelve minutes to five. Today, a ride to the top takes just one minute.

- **Lincoln Memorial.** This profoundly moving memorial to the twelfth president was dedicated in 1922. There are thirty-six columns in the memorial, one for each state in existence at the time of Lincoln's death.

- **Bureau of Engraving and Printing.** Take a tour of the facility where paper currency, postage stamps, and bonds are designed and printed. Sorry, no free samples.

- **Smithsonian Institution.** With fourteen museums and galleries in Washington D.C., the Smithsonian Institution is bound to have something of interest for every member of the family. Charles Lindbergh's *Spirit of St. Louis*, Dorothy's ruby slippers from the *Wizard of Oz*, a woolly mammoth skeleton, the Hope diamond, and the flag that inspired the "Star-Spangled Banner," are just a few of the things in the Smithsonian's collection of more than 140 million items. Don't forget the Air and Space Museum; although major renovations during 2001 have closed many exhibits, others are still open; check them out at the museum's website: www.nasm.edu.

- **National Zoological Park.** Stop by and say hello to Mei Xiang and Tian Tian, the giant pandas on loan from China. The National Zoo is one of only three zoos in the United States where you can see giant pandas. And don't miss the great ape exhibit where the primates have free rein. The rest of the zoo is a winner, too! Check out the zoo's live animal cameras at their website: www.natzoo.si.edu.

- **Mount Vernon.** Just a short drive from downtown D.C. is Mount Vernon, plantation home of George Washington. If you're feeling ambitious, you can bike from D.C. to Mount Vernon on a woodsy bike path. Once you get there, you can tour the mansion and the grounds; just outside the front gate is a snack bar and restaurant.

- **Potomac River Cruises.** A host of companies offer dinner cruises along the Potomac to Mount Vernon.

Check out Spirit Cruises (www.spiritofwashington.com) or Capitol River Cruises (www.gwjapan.com/crc).

Many attractions, including tours of government buildings, are free, but some tours require tickets or reservations. Call ahead to find out the details.

If you're thinking about a trip to Washington, D.C., contact the offices of your U.S. senators or representatives for some good general information about places to go and things to see during your visit. In addition, your congressperson may be able to make reservations or help you get tickets for tours of government facilities.

If your child is older, consider a visit to the U.S. Supreme Court while it's in session—you can actually watch lawyers present the cases. Or check out the *Washington Post* to find out where and when committee hearings are being held on Capitol Hill that day. Hearings are held in small rooms on the Hill and are open to the public—you'll be able to watch even the most famous congressman or congresswoman up-close and in action. It's a much more intimate look at how government works.

63

Every kid should have a secret hideout.

Children of all ages love the idea of having a secret hideout; a place where they can hang out with their best friends, or a place to go and just be alone. Even the youngest children will drag favorite possessions under a card table covered with a blanket and stay there for hours.

If you have the room (maybe in the basement), collect a variety of washer, dryer, stove, and refrigerator boxes from local appliance stores. Help your child to arrange the boxes in the perfect layout. Use a utility knife to cut openings between the rooms, and attach them together with duct tape. Decorate inside and out with acrylic craft paint.

If you are really ambitious and handy with a hammer and saw, consider building your child a more permanent hideout, such as a wooden playhouse for the corner of the backyard or a tree house tucked up in the branches of a huge oak. Buy a set of plans or draw up your own. Before investing time and money in this project, talk to your child about special features. Incorporate as many of the practical requests as possible so that your child will have a truly special place.

To make it even more special, involve your child as much as possible during the building process. Your child can hand you nails, pick up the scraps of lumber, or get each of you a cold glass of lemonade—anything to be involved.

No matter if it's a card table and blanket or a tree house, no hideout would be complete without the following:

- Flashlights, one per person

- Stack of comic books or other favorite reading material

- Popcorn, chips, pretzels, and other snacks

- A deck of cards and a set of checkers

- Large floor pillows, covered in a durable fabric

- A couple of friends who know the secret password

64

Every kid should play classic games.

Unplug the video games, hide the batteries, and teach your child to play all the traditional games you enjoyed as a child. Spend a day playing jump rope, marbles, jacks, charades, pick-up sticks, hopscotch, dominoes, checkers, Go Fish, cat's cradle, I Spy, rock-paper-scissors, pitching pennies, or building a house of cards. If you are a little rusty on the rules, or if you'd like to learn some new games, check your local library for books on traditional games. You might even find a few books with children's games from other countries and cultures. For extra fun, help your child put a personal touch on the games by adding new rules or game pieces to create a custom version. This can give your child a game to call "their own."

Marbles

Available in a rainbow of colors along with a glow-in-the-dark version, polymer clay is a terrific medium for creating homemade marbles. Bake according to the manufacturer's directions on the package.

Pick-Up Sticks

Cut thin dowels or bamboo skewers to the desired length. Sand the ends. Paint the sticks in an assortment of colors, adding stripes, dots, and other decorations. For easier painting, insert the sticks into a piece of foam, paint, and allow them to dry. Remove and stick the painted end into the foam and finish decorating. Remember to paint one stick all black to be used as the pick-up stick.

Hopscotch

Don't let bad weather rain on your hopscotch game; create an indoor version. Cut ten large squares of felt. Decorate each square with a number from one through ten. Add other felt embellishments as desired. Glue a piece of non-skid mat to the bottom of each piece.

Checkers

Use craft foam to create custom checkers pieces. The pieces can be used on a store-bought board, or your child can create a board in a different color scheme using a heavy piece of cardboard.

Dominoes

Using heavy cardboard or thin wood cut into small rectangles, your child can use markers, paints, or stickers to make a set of dominoes featuring a favorite theme.

Cards

Any card game will be more fun with a personalized set of cards. Cut fifty-two pieces of 2½" x 3½" cardstock. Decorate front and back with markers and stickers.

65

Every kid should run a lemonade stand.

Lynn Arnold
Administrative Assistant to the Head of the Lower School
Lancaster, PA

Some of the biggest entrepreneurs of past generations may have gotten their first business experience running a lemonade stand. Perhaps you spent a few hot summer afternoons sitting on the curb, hoping to sell a glass or two to a neighbor. Unfortunately, it's no longer always safe for kids to sit on the curb or in the front yard selling this classic summer drink, but that doesn't mean your child can't share in this experience. It will just take a little work and creativity.

If you or someone you know is planning to have a garage sale, consider letting your child set up a lemonade stand at the sale. If it's not your own sale, volunteer to help out and keep an eye on the lemonade stand at the same time. Another alternative is to help your child and a group of friends set up a table at a school, church, or community fundraising event. Encourage the kids to donate some or all of their profits to the cause.

Whichever option you and your child choose, be sure to be well prepared. Have your child create a large, colorful sign for the front of the stand or table, and have plenty of disposable cups, ice, change, and, of course, homemade lemonade on hand.

Old-Fashioned Lemonade

Ingredients
6 lemons

3 cups water

1–1½ cups sugar syrup (see below)

Squeeze the juice from the lemons. Mix well with the sugar syrup and water. Serve very cold.

Sugar Syrup

Boil four cups of sugar and four cups of water together for ten minutes. Pour into a jar and refrigerate.

Or, if you have a line of thirsty customers, try this quick and easy alternative.

Quick Lemonade

Ingredients

1 cup sugar
1 cup fresh lemon juice
5 cups water
lemon slices (for garnish)

Mix together all ingredients. Stir well to dissolve the sugar. Serve over ice, garnish with lemon slices.

66

Every kid should mark birthdays with a celebration.

Whether it's a simple sleepover with a best friend or a big bash for everyone in the class, do something special to make your child's birthday memorable.

Help your child select a theme for the event. Brainstorm to come up with as many ideas related to the theme as possible, everything from invitations to decorations to take-home gifts. Try: space, magic, fairyland, medieval castle, *101 Dalmatians*, dinosaurs, wild animals, cowboy/cowgirls, Candyland, a backwards party, and so on.

If your house or yard isn't large enough to accommodate all of the guests or if you just don't have time to get them ready for a party, check into other options. Parks, bowling alleys, and skating rinks often rent their facilities for parties. Best of all, there's not much cleanup after the party's over.

Make sleepover guests feel right at home with personalized pillowcases. Buy plain, white pillowcases and jazz them up with permanent craft and fabric markers. To make the decorating easier, cut a piece of heavy cardboard the same size as the pillowcase, and slip it inside the pillowcase. You want a tight fit. For best results, follow the manufacturer's directions on the markers.

This is also a great activity to do *at* the party—let the guests decorate their own pillowcases; and if they do get any sleep that night, they'll definitely have sweet dreams.

Make your own sundaes: here's an activity everybody can enjoy! Line up containers filled with add-ons: chocolate sauce, fudge sauce, M&Ms, nuts, coconut, banana slices, chocolate or colored sprinkles, thin pretzel sticks, and cherries.

Don't cry over popped balloons. Instead, add a small treat so that after the balloon has popped, the fun has just begun. Before blowing up the balloons (or having them blown up by a helium tank), put some glitter or confetti, a small piece of candy, a small plastic toy, or a joke or riddle written on a small scroll into the balloon. There won't be any unpopped balloons left lying around when the party is over—guaranteed.

Buy some good-quality face paint, and let the kids paint each other's faces.

Make your own pizza. Buy small pita or pocket-bread shells. Give one to each child, and build individual pizzas using a selection of toppings: tomato sauce, pepperoni, hamburger, peppers, mushrooms, onions, olives, pineapple, and cheese. Heat until the cheese is melted and eat.

If, like most kids, your child already has enough toys to last several lifetimes, ask guests to bring a toy that will be donated to a local shelter or agency. Let parents know ahead of time that you'll be doing this so guests don't spend hours deciding on the perfect present for *your* child, only to find out that it's going to be donated.

Ask each child to bring a small treat (food or small toy) to share with everyone invited to the party. When you do this, the guests help you create the take-home presents.

67

Every kid should clown around.

Most children are natural-born performers. They don't worry too much about what other people think of them, and they pride themselves in being goofy and making other people laugh. Who better to become an honest-to-goodness clown?

Just about every clown has a gimmick. Before embarking on clown training, help your clowns-in-training investigate their own ideas, such as:

- Juggling

- Making balloon animals

- Simple magic

- Face painting

- Equipment (big shoes, water-squirting flowers, or an invisible dog leash)

- Miming

- Voice throwing or ventriloquism

Start with a trip to the library and check out a few books on the gimmicks that interest your child. Then try to find someone to help your child master and perfect that gimmick.

For real clown training in makeup, costumes, stunts, and other tricks, check with local community or enrichment education for classes on how to become a clown, or check out local clown organizations in your area. If you can't find clown classes for your child, ask a clown you meet at a birthday party or a carnival. They might know where to find training or organizations. In addition to teaching your child the tricks of the trade, a local organization will most likely be able to offer suggestions and advice on gimmicks and obtaining costumes and props. Consider attending the classes and meetings with your child, as you will most likely be called upon to help with hair, makeup, and costuming.

When siblings have had enough of the whole clown act, suggest that your clown branch out. Look into the possibility of performing at school carnivals, senior centers or nursing homes, church functions, the children's ward at the hospital, and the birthday parties of family, friends, and neighbors.

68

Every kid should go to a family reunion.

John Bontumasi
Sales
Flint, MI

When you flip through the family photo albums, how many of the people can your child identify? Has your child ever met your Uncle Joe, the uncle you spent a week with each summer? What about your cousin Anna? Even though you were a few years younger, she was always willing to let you tag along, and she'd even let you try on her newest shade of lipstick. Depending on geographic distances between relatives, your child might not even know your aunts, uncles, and cousins. If that's the case, maybe it's time for a family reunion.

Set a date and start planning. Give everyone as much notice as possible, especially people who will be traveling a considerable distance. If you have a large extended family, enlist the help of several other family members, and assign everyone a specific task. Involve your children as much as possible. If they are too young to take on actual responsibilities, keep them updated on all the latest news and plans.

Consider renting a pavilion at a park or a hall so you have enough room for everyone. That way, no one will feel pressured to get the house or yard ready for a large gathering.

To show your child how everyone fits into the family, work together to create a family tree. Start with a rough draft, and when you have all the details filled in, create a large, display-sized version for the reunion so that everyone can see who is related to whom, and how. If possible, include current pictures so that people can put faces and names together.

Have your child design a special T-shirt for the occasion. Scan the image and do transfers on your home computer, or have the shirts professionally printed. Instead of name tags, personalize each shirt using a permanent craft or fabric marker.

Plan a variety of different games and activities, the cornier the better. Have a talent show—everyone *must* do some sort of act in the show.

During the reunion, give each child a camera and assign the task of interviewing one unfamiliar family member. After the reunion, collect the interviews and cameras. Type up the interviews, get the photos developed, and create a memory booklet. Send a copy to each family. Remember to send a copy to those who were unable to attend.

69

Every kid should make a pizza.

Does your child think that pizza either comes from the freezer section of the grocery store or from the pizza delivery person? If so, it's definitely time to make a personal pizza. Picking up the phone to order a pizza or popping a frozen pizza in the oven is quick and easy, but making a pizza at home is fun. By using a store-bought, prebaked crust, it really doesn't take any longer than delivery.

In addition to a crust, pick up a variety of your family's favorite pizza toppings. Many traditional pizza toppings are available in packages where they are clean, cut up, and ready to go. If not, you'll have to clean and cut up the things your family wants on the pizza. This is the most time-consuming part of homemade pizza. Experiment with a variety of different toppings, sauces, and cheeses until you find your family's favorite combination.

Short on ideas? Collect take-out menus from local restaurants and pizzerias for inspiration. Working together as a family to create a masterpiece is part of the fun of making pizza, but if your family can't agree on toppings, provide everyone with a small, individual crust and let everyone make a mini-masterpiece.

If your child is convinced that the best pizza comes from out of a cardboard box, check with area pizzerias to see if you can purchase empty boxes. Then, after you've baked *your* pizza, transfer it to the box for serving.

Your family may enjoy making pizza so much that it becomes a weekly dinner event. And who knows, maybe one day you'll try making a hand-tossed crust for the pizza. When you are ready to give it a try, here's a terrific homemade crust recipe:

Homemade Pizza Crust

Ingredients

2–2¼ cups all-purpose white flour

1 pkg. RapidRise yeast

1 tsp. salt

½ tsp. sugar

¾ cup very warm tap water (120–130°F)

1 tsp. olive oil

1. In a large mixing bowl, stir together 1½ cups flour, yeast, salt, and sugar.

2. Stir the oil and water into the flour. Beat until well mixed.

3. Gradually add enough of the remaining flour to make a firm, soft dough.

4. Turn out onto a lightly floured surface and knead until smooth and elastic.

5. Cover with plastic and let rest for 10 minutes.

6. Preheat oven to 425°F.

7. Form dough into crust shape on a large cookie sheet.

8. Add sauce and toppings.

9. Bake for 15 to 20 minutes or until the crust is crisp and brown.

Makes four 6-inch crusts, or one large crust.

70

Every kid should learn to appreciate the different abilities of people.

When children see someone walking with a guide dog, communicating in sign language, or riding in a wheelchair, they often stare—not because they are rude, but because they are simply curious. This is the perfect time to teach your child about the abilities of differently abled people.

Kids are fascinated with sign language, and they can learn to sign at a very early age. For children who are interested, kindergarten/first grade is the perfect time to start to learn to fingerspell. You can teach the letters one-by-one, and the child can practice spelling reading words and other short words. If your child likes fingerspelling and is interested in learning more, suggest a sign language class. Check with community education or continuing education programs, recreation and community centers, libraries, religious organizations, hearing impaired–related organizations, and community colleges or universities for classes that would be appropriate for you and your child. If you have the chance, check out a performance by the national touring company of The National Theatre of the Deaf, which specializes in performing plays in sign language.

Children are also fascinated by seeing-eye dogs. When you encounter a guide dog, remind your child that the dog is working and should not be disturbed—no petting! But if the opportunity presents itself, encourage your child to ask the owner questions about the dog. Most are more than happy to talk about their guide dog and how it helps them handle everyday tasks sighted people take for granted.

Many children are fascinated about secret codes; introduce your child to braille, a system of raised dots used by blind people to read. Your child can practice by making the letters of the alphabet, numbers, and punctuation marks with pencil and paper. Contact a state school for the blind and see if they would be willing to send you some samples of actual raised braille writing. If it's feasible, see if you can arrange for your child to visit the school and try using a braillewriter.

If you and your child run into someone in a wheelchair, offer some assistance if it's needed. Afterwards, talk to your child about why people need wheelchairs and briefly discuss some of the ways their life is different. Don't dwell on all the things people in wheelchairs *can't* do, but talk about the things they can do. To reinforce this message, take your child to a wheelchair sporting event or a performance of a wheelchair ballet troupe.

Teach your child that any time you encounter someone who is differently abled to treat that person with the same respect and politeness you would offer to anyone.

71

Every kid should be taken for a "pajama ride."

Carol Turkington
Writer
Mohnton, PA

We all get caught up in the busy day-to-day existence. An unexpected treat can be a wonderful change of pace.

Plan your caper for a warm late-spring or early-fall Friday evening. Everyone will have a much more enjoyable time if you choose an evening when your child isn't too tired from a busy day. Shortly after tucking your child in for the night, return to the bedroom, flip on the lights, and announce *"Pajama ride!"* Grab a pair of your child's slippers on your way out. Don't stop to get dressed—going out in pajamas is a big part of this treat!

Pile into the car and head off to a local eatery for banana splits, extra-thick strawberry milkshakes, or a large plate of fries. While the crazy looks your child will get are part of the fun of this adventure, older children might prefer being taken to a location in a neighboring town where there's less of a chance of running into a friend! Or let your child stay in the car while you get the food, if you think there might be some potential embarrassment.

Take your treat to a nearby park, where you can sit outside and watch the stars as you lick your cones or slurp your shakes. Climb back into the car and spend some time driving around. Many younger children have had few opportunities to see the world after dark; they'll enjoy all the colorful signs of the businesses where you shop during daylight hours. Spend the time telling stories, singing songs, or catching up on happenings of the last week. If they don't manage to stay awake until you get home, at least they are ready to be put right back to bed.

Consider wearing your pajamas one night. Your child will probably think it's really neat for the whole family to eat banana splits in their pajamas!

72

Every kid should have a "get better" box.

For a child, the worst part of being sick is being stuck home in bed while other children are at school having fun. They imagine they are missing a really neat project in art class, a killer game of kickball in gym, or a pep assembly for the basketball team.

You can take a little bit of the pain out of being sick with a "get better" box. Prepared before you need it and then tucked away in a closet, you'll be all set the next time someone has a sick day from school.

To create a "get better" box for your child, pack some or all of the following into a small storage tub:

- A "get better" pillowcase. If you can't find a really neat ready-made pillowcase, buy a yard of fabric and sew up one of your own. Or use permanent fabric markers and fabric paint to decorate a plain, store-bought pillowcase.

- A muffin tin. Handy for snacks. Fill the compartments with nuts, raisins, dry cereal, dried fruit, and other healthy snacks.

- Chenille stems, cut into a variety of lengths, and pony beads. Perfect for creating an infinite number of creatures with minimal mess.

- A chalkboard and chalk or whiteboard and dry-erase markers. Practice numbers, letters, or create works of art without the hassle of paper.

- A roll of tape. For some unknown reason, a piece of tape will keep a sick child occupied for hours.

- "Sick socks." A pair of outrageous socks, the wilder the better, guaranteed to make the wearer feel better fast. For a truly special pair of sick socks, see if you can commission a knitter to create a pair for your child.

- Puppets, stickers, comic books, activity books, and a deck of cards.

- No "get better" box would be complete without a "get better" wand. To be used only by adults, the get better wand is endowed with magic powers that are certain to bring a smile to your child's face. To craft a get better wand, glue a wooden star to a dowel, paint it, and attach long, colorful ribbon streamers to the wand.

73

Every kid should blow soap bubbles.

Blowing soap bubbles is the perfect way to spend a balmy spring day or a lazy summer day, and it will be even more fun if your child mixes up the bubble solution. Here's how:

Ingredients

2 tbsp. glycerin (available at most drug stores)

¼ cup dish soap

1 cup water

food coloring (optional)

In a plastic jar, gently stir together the glycerin, dish soap, and water. You can color the mixture with a drop or two of food coloring, but it won't create colored bubbles. This mixtures gets better with age, so mix it up ahead of time if possible.

Then the real fun starts: finding things around the house that can be used to blow the bubbles. To blow giant bubbles, create wands with 12- or 14-gauge, solid, not stranded electrical wire. Electrical wire is readily available, inexpensive, and easy to bend without special tools. Create a variety of wands in different shapes and sizes and see how large a bubble your child can blow.

Or help your child collect a variety of things to make bubbles with:

- Colander

- Slotted kitchen spoons

- Plastic berry baskets

- Old tennis or badminton rackets

- Plastic needlework canvas

- Egg dippers leftover from dyeing Easter eggs

- A piece of window screen (place duct tape around the edges to prevent scratches)

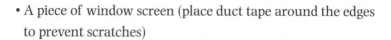

Pour the bubble solution into a shallow pan and try to fill the air with millions of tiny bubbles.

74

Every kid should spend some time alone with each parent.

Marge Graybeal
Library retiree, fiction writer
New Jersey

Just you and your child, spending time together with no interruptions; no big sister asking if she can borrow the car Friday night, no little brother asking for a glass of milk or a cookie, no TV, no telemarketers. It doesn't matter if you're grocery shopping, picking up the dry cleaning, or sharing an ice cream sundae, your child will cherish the opportunity to spend some time with Mom or Dad alone.

For many families, there are only a few hours between the time Mom and Dad get home from work and the time the kids need to go to bed. Those precious few hours are usually spent making dinner, eating, doing dishes and homework, taking a bath, or doing a load of laundry. With sports practice and games, errands, housework, yard work, and other obligations, weekends are no better.

So what's a busy family to do? Make the most of every chance you get to spend a little one-on-one time with your child. Even a trip to the hardware store for a few bolts, or to the grocery store for a gallon of milk, provides time for you to talk to and listen to your child without all the interruptions of your everyday life. Make the most of these opportunities. Stop for an ice cream when the errands are done. Share a laugh about getting caught in the rain without an umbrella. Plan some special parent-child times as well. Regardless of what you do, your child will cherish those "Mom/Dad and me" times:

- Pick your child up from school one afternoon and head to a favorite bakery or restaurant for a special after-school snack. Finish the afternoon with a trip to the park.

- Plan a Saturday in the city. Head out early in the morning for a day of shopping, visit the museum, or catch a matinee.

- Go for a long walk or bike ride.

196

- Send the rest of the family off for the day and spend a day at home, just you and your child. Paint your child's bedroom, plant a garden, or spend the day working on a shared project or hobby.

75

Every kid should build a model.

Most children have at least one passionate interest. It might be a fascination with cars, airplanes, ships, or ponies—whatever it is, one excellent way for both you and your child to learn more about this interest is to build a model.

Kits are available at any toy store or hobby store for many of the things kids are interested in building. You can get all kinds of model kits:

- Ships

- Trains

- Planes

- Cars

- Rocket ships and spacecrafts

- Human body (anatomy)

- Human skull

- Body of a horse

- Egyptian mummy

- Dollhouses

- Dinosaurs

- Tanks and artillery

- Pirate ships

- Military men

- Action figures

These projects are usually available at several levels of difficulty, so you can match the right project to your child's age and ability. If your child is old enough and has the skill to complete the project without help from you, try to stay involved in the process by discussing it. If your child is working on something that's outside your area of expertise, do some research so that you can discuss the different parts of the model intelligently. Be sure to proudly display the finished product.

Don't let the fact that your child isn't interested in any of the "traditional" model kits stop you from suggesting a related model.

A child interested in mythology and dragons might research and build a medieval castle. A child in love with horses may like the idea of building a stable for a collection of model ponies.

Building a model of something is also an excellent teaching tool. If your child is presented with an opportunity to earn some extra credit, suggest a model related to the theme of the unit instead of the standard book report. In order to really do a good job on the model, your child will need to become somewhat of an expert on the topic, whether it's a wigwam, a tepee, a birch-bark canoe, a log cabin, a bridge, or the Eiffel tower. When all is said and done, your child may forget the grade that he received, but he will never forget building the model.

76

Every kid should go on a scavenger hunt.

Kids (especially older ones) will tell you that they are very observant—nothing gets past them. But just how sharp-eyed are they really? Collect a group of neighborhood kids and put their skills to the test. Here's how to set up a scavenger hunt:

1. First you'll have to put your own skills to the test. Establish some boundaries within the neighborhood and then head out to see what you can see within those boundaries. The items you saw on your tour will be included on the lists of "things to find." How many items you include will depend on your child's age. A good rule of thumb is to link the number of items to your child's age.

2. Make a list of "things to find": a nut, a yellow leaf, pine cone, and so on.

3. Send the kids out in teams of two or more, armed with a list of "things to find."

4. Make the boundaries clear, and set a time limit.

5. Reward *all* the teams with cookies, ice cream, or pizza.

After your child has had some practice, consider involving the whole family in a road rally/scavenger hunt. Here's how:

1. Prepare several puzzles, riddles, and/or coded messages to serve as the clues.

2. Arrange to plant clues at area businesses or at the homes of family and friends.

3. Start at home with one clue. When the puzzle, riddle, or message is deciphered, it will reveal the location of the next clue.

4. After several stops with new sets of clues, conclude the road rally/scavenger hunt at a local bowling alley, miniature golf center, or favorite restaurant for a treat or an afternoon of family fun.

77

Every kid should go to a baseball game with Grandpa.

Kevin Hohf
College student
Chesterfield, MI

Enjoying hot dogs while watching a baseball game on a warm spring or summer afternoon is a perfect experience for any child. Make the experience even more special by arranging for your child to share it with a grandparent, aunt or uncle, or some other adult instead of Mom or Dad.

By sharing the experience with a grandparent or another significant adult, your child will have an opportunity to not only share an afternoon, but strengthen intergenerational ties. Sometimes it's just nice for a child to chat with an adult other than Mom or Dad.

It doesn't have to be a baseball game. If your child isn't really interested in baseball, arrange for tickets to a horse show, basketball or football game, or ice hockey playoff. The experience will be much more memorable and enjoyable if you choose a team or sport that interests your child.

If a professional event is too far away or costs too much, consider attending a local college or minor-league team. Tickets for these games are usually inexpensive, and since they typically play in much smaller stadiums, your child will have a better chance of enjoying the action of the game up close.

78

Every kid should play with his food.

You can make any meal more enjoyable with a variety of creative and crazy foods. Ask for your child's input and help, and the results may be almost too fun to eat!

Cookie cutters can make breakfast, lunch, dinner, and even snack time more fun. For fun sandwiches, use large cookie cutters to cut bread into a variety of shapes for fun sandwiches. Next, cut meat or cheese with smaller cookie cutters before assembling the sandwich. Cookie cutters can also be used to cut shapes in pancakes, French toast, brownies, or sheet cakes, or as molds for scrambled eggs or chicken salad.

Make any meal more festive with color. Use food coloring to serve pink milk on Valentine's Day, green mashed potatoes on

St. Patrick's Day, or to create a homemade version of Neapolitan ice cream featuring red, white, and blue for the Fourth of July.

Make kabobs using toothpicks and skewers and a variety of fresh fruits and vegetables cut into pieces to create unique and refreshing after-school snacks.

Form store-bought, ready-to-bake breadsticks into hearts, rings, numbers, letters of the alphabet, or even stick people. Bake according to the directions on the package.

Any food is more fun when you dip it. Fill several small, plastic condiment cups with ketchup, mustard, honey, barbecue sauce, sweet and sour sauce, and ranch salad dressing (or other family favorite), and let your child dip dinner.

Make faces. Using the bottom of a bun as the foundation for a face, let your child create a wild, out-of-this-world, edible creature. Depending on your child's vision, and what supplies you have available, the creation may feature a bologna complexion, cherry-tomato or black-olive eyes framed by mustard spectacles, bean or broccoli-sprout hair, a green-pepper grin, apple-slice ears with raisin earrings, and celery or carrot-stick antennae. When the creature is complete, let your child eat it as an open-faced sand-wich, or put the top on for a total meal.

79

Every kid should see Mom or Dad laugh.

With all the stress of work, the responsibilities of raising a family, the pressure to make sure everyone gets where they need to be when they need to be there, and well, just being a grown-up, parents don't laugh nearly as much as they did when they were children. Try and find an opportunity each day to laugh with your children:

- Rent the silliest, goofiest, funniest family-oriented movie you can find (maybe one of your childhood favorites) and watch it with your child.

- Laugh at your child's jokes, no matter how many times you have heard them. Think back to grade school when you told that same joke at least once a day. Learn a few equally corny jokes to share with your child.

- Read the funny pages together every day.

- Have a competition with your child to see who can make the silliest face.

- Tickle each other.

- Have a pillow fight.

- Stand in the middle of the mall with your child and stare up at the ceiling. Giggle at the people who walk by wondering what in the world you're looking at.

- Have a staring contest. See what you can do to make your competition crack a smile.

- Skip through the grocery store.

- Spend a hot summer afternoon throwing water balloons at one another.

- Work together to rewrite the words of a current, popular song with your own crazy lyrics.

80

Every kid should make caramel apples.

Norma Testa
Executive Director
Wilmington, DE

There's something special about the early days of October, with bright blue skies and puffy, white clouds. School is still new and exciting, full of hope and anticipation for the year ahead. New friends are being made. And most of the crayons in that box bought just for school are still in one piece. Saturday afternoons are reserved for raking leaves into a big pile, jumping in, and then starting all over again. The anticipation of Halloween hangs heavy in the air. In many areas it's time to harvest apples, so head off to your local orchard or grocery store and stock up on apples and caramel, and make a batch of these fabulous fall favorites.

Caramel Apple Recipe

Ingredients

1 cup chopped peanuts (optional)

6 apples

14-oz. package of caramel candies

2 tbsp. milk

1. Butter a baking sheet and set aside.

2. Chop about a cup of peanuts and set aside. If you have a child-safe chopper, this is a job your child can do.

3. Remove the stems from the apples, wash and dry them well, and insert a craft or lollipop stick into each apple.

4. Unwrap caramels and place in a microwave-safe bowl. Add milk and microwave for 2 minutes, stirring once. Let cool briefly.

5. Dip the apples into the melted caramel one at a time, quickly turning the apple until it is completely coated. Dip the apple into the nuts and set it on the baking sheet.

6. Set the apples aside until they are cool, and then enjoy.

81

Every kid should publish a book.

Picture yourself sitting with your grandchildren, reading to them a book that their Mom or Dad wrote and illustrated as a child. In order to make this vision a reality, you'll first need to find a place that will bind the masterpiece once it's complete.

Some children's toy stores and catalogs offer kits that allow you to create a one-of-a-kind hardbound book. These kits contain specific guidelines for your child to follow. For more information on book kits, contact Recollections Keepsake Books ((800) 432-8290 or www.erecollections.com).

If you can't find such a kit, check with local print shops to see if they offer this service or can refer you to someplace that does. If you have a college or university in your area, contact them to see who does the binding for their theses and dissertations. Call and see if they would be willing to bind your child's book. If you can find a source to bind the book, you'll need to supply your child with paper and other supplies to complete the project. When buying paper, look for a good-quality, acid-free, heavy, bright-white paper, twenty-four-pound or cardstock. For ease of reading in the future, consider suggesting that your child write the text of the final version on a computer.

After the text has been printed, your child can add illustrations using acid-free colored pencils or pens that won't smear, smudge, or fade over the years.

Before sending the book off to be bound, make sure that your child has included a title page, acknowledgments, a dedication, and of course, an "About the Author" page.

82

Every kid should have a best friend.

Make new friends but keep the old,
One is silver and the other gold.
A circle's round, it has no end,
That's how long I want to be your friend.
—Author unknown

As this old scouting song reminds us, friendship is a big part of childhood. Having friends seems like the most natural thing in the world for a kid. After all, they spend all day together in the classroom, eating lunch, and playing on the playground. But sometimes kids need a little help from Mom or Dad to turn an everyday acquaintance into a friend.

Because they have a pool of potential friends to pick from, it will be easier to help a school-aged child foster a friendship than it will be to help a younger child make friends. Talk to your child about

213

playmates at school, and set up a one-on-one play date with one of those children. Just one child is a good number; having more than one child over to play with involves the risk of someone feeling excluded from the rest of the group.

It might take a couple of play dates before you can determine whether or not the friendship will "take." It might take several tries before your child finds a friend that matches up with similar hobbies, interests, likes, and dislikes.

For younger children with no siblings (or siblings too young to be playmates), you might have to work harder to find friends. Other neighborhood children are always a good place to start looking for friends because of the convenience of having a playmate across the street, next door, or down the block. If that isn't an option, look around your community for playgroups, story times, art classes, gymnastics lessons, and other opportunities for you and your child to meet other parents and children. Plan some one-on-one time with parents and children with whom you and your child connect. With a little work, you might have the beginnings of a lifelong friendship.

83

Every kid should experience the feelings of love, safety, and security.

Bella Brattkull
Dietician
Gothenburg, Sweden

Every parent gets caught up in the reality of everyday life; relax a little and spend some time with your child! The laundry and the lawn will still be there tomorrow, so take some time *today*, and every day, to make sure your child feels safe, secure, and loved.

- Never let the sun set without having told your child at *least* once, "I love you."

- Really *listen* to your child.

- Slip a note under your child's pillow, or into her underwear drawer, letting her know that she's loved and appreciated. "Do you know what I like about you? I like it when you..."

- Enjoy your child: fill your home with smiles, love, laughter, and a bit of craziness.

- Hug your child: as kids leave toddlerhood behind, we often neglect to keep hugging them, but you *never* outgrow your need for hugs.

- At least once a day, tell your child, "I think you're a terrific kid!"

- Never send your child to bed without hugs, kisses, and a check for monsters hiding in the closet and under the bed.

- Don't dismiss your child's fears, no matter how silly they may seem to you. Take time to talk to your child about those fears.

- The next time a thunderstorm wakes your child up, sit with him on the couch and watch the storm. If it looks like it's going to be a long one, pop some popcorn and watch the lightning streak across the sky.

- Cuddle on the couch, because your child is scared, upset, worried, feeling ill, or for no particular reason at all.

84

Every kid should participate in an extracurricular activity.

There's a lot more to school than just what happens in the classroom. After-school activities can provide a wealth of information and opportunities for your child. From scouting to sports, art club, drama club, science club, and reading club, most schools have a wide range of activities from which to choose. One of them is bound to interest your child.

If your school doesn't happen to have an activity that catches your child's interest, talk to the principal about starting a new club. Quite often, extracurricular activities at a school are lacking because of a dearth of volunteers, so offer your time and talents. Consider one of the following:

- **Book Club.** All readers welcome. Each week pick a different theme—dinosaurs, teddy bears, bugs, animals, or football—and encourage members to read books related to the theme. During your after-school meetings, create simple theme-related crafts and eat a theme-related snack. For example, if bugs are the topic, you can snack on "worms and dirt" (chocolate pudding cups sprinkled with gummy worms) while making bug bookmarks. Laminate the finished projects.

- **Walking Club.** All ages welcome for some fun and physical fitness! Before your first club meeting, establish and measure out a walking route (typically a quarter mile or half mile). Set up both indoor and outdoor locations in case of bad weather. Prepare cards with the students' names that you can stamp or punch each time they complete a lap. Have plenty of water available for the walkers. As with any physical activity, obtain parental permission and a doctor's clearance for each of the participants.

- **Craft Club.** Using supplies donated by parents or area businesses, students can stretch their creative wings. Select several quality projects for students to make, and plan to sell the completed items at a school sale. Consider scheduling the sales and projects to coincide with the December holidays, Valentine's Day, Mother's Day, and Father's Day. Any profits from the sales can be put back into the club to buy more supplies.

- **School Paper.** Organize all interested students, and help them scoop "all the news that's fit to print." The cub reporters can interview teachers and other school staff, review movies, and report on individual student and team achievements. Let the students help to assemble the finished product, which you can then have copied at a local print shop. If you're computer savvy and the school has the equipment, you can produce the paper yourself using desktop publishing. Sell the paper (only for enough to cover the copying charges) in the hall between classes or at lunch.

- **Volunteer Club.** Encourage students of all ages to get involved and give back to the school and community. Look around your school—does the playground need some picking up? Are there leaves that need raking or flower beds to be weeded? Is there something that needs to be painted? What about organizing a food drive? If you should happen to run out of projects at school, look into the community for ways to help. Consider "adopting" a local needy family identified by community churches, or gather food for the town food pantry. After a hard day of work, reward volunteers with pizza, ice cream, hamburgers, or hot dogs donated by local merchants.

85

Every kid should have a pen pal.

Learning about people and places around the country or around the world by reading facts and stories in a book is one thing, but getting the information from a firsthand account written by someone your age is a whole different story. Pen pals offer each other the opportunity to learn about life in another place—and the chance to make a friend.

As a child, you may have had a pen pal with whom you exchanged letters. Today, your child is more likely to correspond via the Internet with an e-pal. But before finding your child a new e-friend, spend some time discussing Internet safety. Remind your child to *never* give personal information such as last name, address, phone number, or photographs to *anyone* over the Internet, no matter how good a friend the person seems. Encourage your child to share the messages with you so that you can watch for potential problems. Also, for safety purposes, you might consider setting up a special email account for your child to use when corresponding with e-pals.

Once your child is ready, you can find email pen pals through a number of websites. Many of these sites also have additional safety tips you should share and discuss with your child. To get started, check out a few of the following:

- Kids' Space Connection: www.ks-connection.org

- Kid City Post Office: www.child.net/kcpo.htm

- Kid City Kid's Mailbox (for kids under 13): www.child.net/kids mail.htm

- A Girl's World Pen Pal Club (for girls ages 7–17): www.agirlsworld.com/geri/penpal/index.html

- ePALS Classroom Exchange (for teachers to connect with another classroom): www.epals.com

Encourage your child to write the first letter to the new pen pal. Help your child write a letter that's interesting and inquisitive, discussing school, hobbies, pets, sports, favorite movies, music, and books. Remind your child to ask questions. It will not only help the pen pal with a response, but it will be a way for your child to get specific questions answered.

If you'd like for your child to have a more traditional pen pal experience exchanging letters, contact World Pen Pals at P.O. Box

337, Saugerties, NY 12477 or (845)246-7828. Note: World Pen Pals charges a small fee for their service.

Regardless of what type of pen friend you find, remind your child that the pen pal is also busy and will write as soon as possible. If your child doesn't get a reply after a sufficient amount of time, suggest writing another letter. Keep in mind that mail, even email, does get lost and misdirected. If the pen pal relationship doesn't work out, try to locate another partner for your child.

In order to get the most out of the experience, help your child learn about the place where the pen pal lives. Locate the pen pal's town on a map and learn a little bit about the history and culture of the area.

86

Every kid should have a personal library card.

Becky Ballance
Elementary school teacher
Goodrich, MI

With a simple piece of cardboard or plastic, you can open the world to your child...go to places you'd never be able to visit in person, travel back in time, or look ahead to the future. All that and so much more is possible with a library card.

One of the first libraries in the country was organized by Benjamin Franklin in the 1730s—but it was a subscription library supported by dues-paying members. The first tax-supported library didn't open until about one hundred years later.

Of course, the king of American libraries is the Library of Congress. Established in 1800, it was intended to be a research library for the members of Congress. Originally housed in the Capitol, the original collection was destroyed when the British burned the building during the War of 1812. To rebuild the library, Congress bought the private collection of Thomas Jefferson, which numbered about six thousand volumes. Today, the Library of Congress is the largest library in the world, containing about 120 million items—including a copy of the Gutenberg Bible.

You may not have the resources of the Library of Congress in your backyard, but most communities have access to some type of library. No single library has the resources to acquire every book in print, or the space to keep every newspaper or magazine they receive—so as a result, libraries share items between themselves. If your library doesn't have an item you want or need, ask about the possibilities of obtaining it through inter-library loan.

87

Every kid should enjoy lazy summer days.

Summer is the perfect time to be a kid. No school, no homework, no responsibilities, and all the time in the world. Time to:

- Stay up way past bedtime, and then sleep in the next morning.

- Eat an ice cream cone, an ice pop, a snow cone, or a big, juicy piece of watermelon, not caring how much it drips or how big a mess it makes.

- Spend an afternoon swinging on a swing.

- Run through the sprinkler or lie around in a shallow wading pool.

- Pick vegetables from the garden, rinse them off with the hose, and chow down.

- Eat a peanut butter and jelly sandwich in the shade of a large tree and then take an afternoon nap there.

- Find an anthill full of busy ants, and spend hours watching them with a magnifying glass, studying everything that they do. (Be sure to keep the magnifying glass at a safe distance from the ground.)

- Chase butterflies.

- Lie on a blanket in the cool grass, looking for shapes in the clouds.

- Climb high into a tree and sit there for hours.

- Do *absolutely nothing.*

88

Every kid should experience the ocean.

Covering more than 70 percent of the earth's surface area, the ocean is an amazing and wonderful world for both you and your child to explore. And, with 4,993 miles of ocean coastline in the contiguous United States, you have a number of options for discovering this water wonderland.

Children are fascinated with sea creatures. Before your trip, study up on the animals that live there: whales, dolphins, seals, manatees, sharks, octopi, lobsters, and fish. Focus on the animals that inhabit the area you'll be visiting.

Seashells picked up along the beach make nice souvenirs. Remember to bring along a plastic pail to collect your child's treasures.

If your child is very young, bring along a small inflatable baby pool. Fill the pool with some buckets of seawater and let your little one play safely in the pool, beside you on the sand.

For unique keepsakes, rent or borrow a metal detector; you never know what you'll uncover.

Try a beach scavenger hunt: give each child a list of items to find, such as five white shells, two shells bigger than a quarter, three shells smaller than a dime, two black shells, and a shell with a hole in it.

If you and your children are fairly experienced swimmers who don't mind having your faces in the water, try snorkeling. If you're just beginners, that's OK, too—you can snorkel in waist-deep water; just bend over, put your face in the water, and enjoy!

Play sand golf. Bury three paper cups in the sand. Have your kids roll golf balls into the cups; first one to sink all the balls wins!

Get your child an inexpensive, disposable underwater camera. Your child will be able to capture some wonderful pictures!

Before you leave home, cut a plastic two-liter soda bottle in half. Let your child use the bottom half to form walls for sand castles; the top half makes a great funnel for pouring seawater!

89

Every kid should be given a camera to take pictures, and the freedom to take whatever pictures she wants to take.

Stacy MacLaren
Homemaker
Tucson, AZ

A photo album filled with blurry and off-center images of rather mundane subjects: why would anyone save and even archive such a collection of mismatched photos? Because, they represent life through the eyes of a child.

To help your budding photo-artist document life, buy an easy-to-use, no-frills camera. Look for a model with a large viewfinder to increase the chances of your child's subject actually appearing in the photo. Also look for a model with a film door that requires two simultaneous actions to open. The harder it is to open the film door, the less pictures your child will lose to prematurely exposed film.

Because children are impatient by nature, consider buying an instant camera. Half the fun of taking pictures with an instant camera is watching the photos appear right before your eyes, and if the photo doesn't turn out like your child had hoped, there's still an opportunity to try and capture the picture again. (Of course, with a digital camera you can tell right away whether the picture turned out well.)

Photography doesn't have to be an expensive hobby. Until your child has mastered the techniques, you don't need to get the best equipment, film, or photo developing. Encourage your child to bring the camera wherever you go, and take pictures of anything. Suggest things like:

• Dad cleaning up after dinner

• Stuffed animals sitting in a neat row on the couch

- Mom working in the garden

- Her bedroom

- A best friend doing anything

- A kitten sleeping in a sunbeam

- Little sister on the potty chair

- The dog eating its dinner

- Big brother doing homework

- Cows grazing in a field

- A flock of starlings dining at the feeder in the backyard

- Dandelions growing in the yard

90

Every kid should produce a video.

Every great film starts with a great story. If your child isn't sure where to start, you might suggest an adaptation of a favorite story. Consider taking a trip to the library to check out a play written specifically for children. Or have your child write the script! Once the story has been selected, it's time to begin:

- **Cast.** Ask friends or family to join the fun. If your child can't find enough people for all the roles, or if that is just too much of an undertaking, use puppets or stuffed animals for some of the characters.

- **Makeup.** In the tradition of true Hollywood classics, use makeup, hair, and costumes to help create the characters.

- **Sound Effects.** Have fun with sound effects. Don't neglect adding a sound when it will enhance the action; a knock on the door, a door slamming, wind chimes, running water. If you can't get the actual sound, challenge your child to come up with an alternative—rice in a dry plastic bottle for a rain shower, popcorn for a heavier shower, or a rock in a covered plastic food-storage container to simulate thunder. With a little effort, your child will probably be able to come up with the perfect effect to create just about any sound.

If your child is old enough to operate the video camera and would rather be behind the camera than in front of it, give it a whirl! Let your child try filming the action. Otherwise, you can film it.

Regardless of who films the production, use a tripod to make the job easier.

After the movie is finished, send out invitations to everyone involved for a premiere party. Pop lots of popcorn and have plenty of soft drinks on hand.

After the premiere of the movie, present your child with a statue or trophy to commemorate the occasion. Maybe one day "Oscar" will join that statue or trophy on your child's mantel. "I'd like to thank The Academy, and my parents, for making this possible…"

91

Every kid should experience the mystery of magic.

Remember the fun of watching a magician pull a rabbit out of his hat and then turning it into a dove? Wondering how the magician can take a severed rope and make it whole again with a tap of his wand? Remember the heart-pounding feeling while the magician cuts his assistant in half?

Show off your own magical abilities and entertain your child by performing several tricks you've learned. Although a true magician never gives away the secrets behind the tricks, it's OK to break the rules with your child. Perform your tricks several times and challenge your child to figure out how they're done. If your child can't figure it out, explain it and show how it's done, step by step. To get your child started, here are a few simple, easy-to-learn tricks.

Mind Reader

Before the show, *tear* (don't cut) a sheet of paper into three strips about the same size.

During the show, ask for three volunteers from the audience. Give a piece of paper and pencil to each and ask each volunteer to write down a favorite food, color, or number. Pay attention to which volunteer has the paper with two ripped edges.

Instruct each volunteer to fold the strip of paper in half lengthwise twice. Put all the papers into the magic top hat. The volunteers can return to their seats.

Walk through the audience, stopping at the person whose paper was ripped on both sides. Put your hands on the person's head and say: "Concentrate on what you wrote on the paper while I read your mind."

Return to the front of the room and remove the paper with the two torn sides from the hat and read what is written on the paper. Confirm with the audience member that it is in fact the correct answer.

The Indestructible Balloon

Before the show, blow up two identical balloons. To one of the balloons, attach two or three *small* pieces of invisible tape. You will also need several straight pins to perform this trick.

As the trick begins, explain to the audience that you have two identical balloons, but with your magical powers you will make one of the balloons indestructible. To prove that the balloons are just ordinary balloons, stick a pin into the balloon that does *not* have the tape on it.

Wave your wand over the remaining balloon (the one with tape) while reciting, "Hocus Pocus. Alakazam. I turn you from an ordinary balloon into a balloon of steel." Gently tap the balloon with the wand.

Carefully insert a pin into a spot on the balloon that is taped. Repeat one or two more times. Show the audience that the pins are actually stuck in the balloon, but don't let them look too closely, or they might notice the tape.

Remove the pins and return the balloon to its normal state with a tap of your wand. Show the audience that the balloon has been restored to normal by inserting a pin into it at a spot that is not taped. (The balloon will pop.)

There are books full of magic tricks available at your local bookstore or library, but as you may have found while learning your tricks, some illusions are difficult to master with only a set of instructions from a book to follow. If your child is interested in learning more tricks, try to locate a shop in your area that sells magic supplies, with a shop owner who can help explain the subtleties of the illusions. Also consider checking for a community enrichment class in magic.

Once your child has mastered several tricks, assemble a few family members, neighbors, and friends for a show. To make sure your future Houdini is properly outfitted for the occasion, surprise your child with a cape sewn from a remnant of black fabric, a wand cut from a dowel painted black with white tips, and a top hat found at a local thrift shop.

92

Every kid should go to summer camp.

Sleeping bags...Arts and crafts...Cabins with bunk beds...
Swimming in the lake...Pangs of homesickness...Roasting marshmallows
over an open fire...New best friends.

The first step to selecting the perfect summer camp for your child is to sit down and look at what type of situation would work best for your child and family—a local day camp or a residential situation?

Next, what type of camp would your child like? Hobbies may provide the answer here: cheerleading, horseback riding, golf, or football skills? Would your daughter like to learn a foreign language, or does your son need to spend some time strengthening math, reading, or science skills? Is your child interested in art, music, or performing arts? Or does your child have a special need, such as asthma, diabetes, epilepsy, or a physical or developmental disability? Believe it or not, there are camps for all these situations—and many, many more.

The Internet is an excellent resource for locating summer camps of all types. For thousands of summer camp opportunities, check out: www.summercamps.com and www.KidsCamps.com.

If for some reason you can't find a camp that fits your needs, try using an Internet search engine (such as www.google.com or www.metacrawler.com), using the keywords "summer camp" along with an appropriate modifier such as "field hockey," "swimming," or "dance." To find camps in your area, be sure to include your state.

93

Every kid should make a meal for the family.

It doesn't matter if it's a simple bowl of cereal, scrambled eggs, or homemade waffles, for some reason children take great delight in preparing breakfast in bed for their parents. Maybe it's the novelty of climbing into bed with them and eating all the best stuff on the tray, or maybe it's their way of saying a special thanks to Mom and Dad for everything they do.

With some help from you, even the youngest child can take pride in serving up a special meal. Your child may want to prepare a special breakfast for a sibling celebrating a birthday or stuck in bed with the chicken pox, or to make lunch or dinner for the entire family. While it might mean eating really messy peanut butter and jelly sandwiches, let your child make them.

241

Even if they haven't spent much time in the kitchen, older kids can manage a lot more than a box of macaroni and cheese. Look through a cookbook with your child to find a few recipes that sound interesting enough. If you don't have a children's cookbook on hand, help your child select recipes that require only minimal help from you.

Make it your child's responsibility to make a list of all ingredients that you don't have in the pantry, and then go shopping together to buy supplies. Back in the kitchen, unless your child asks for help, don't intervene—although you might choose to do preparation that involves a sharp knife, the oven, or the stovetop.

When the meal is finished, have the rest of the family clear the table and do the dishes so that the chef can have a well-deserved rest.

Here are some easy recipes for your child to try:

Pizza Over Easy

Ingredients

1 lb hamburger
15-oz. jar of spaghetti sauce
2 cups shredded mozzarella cheese
1 tube of crescent rolls
1 cup grated Parmesan cheese

1. Preheat oven to $350°$F.

2. Brown meat in skillet, stirring until crumbly.

3. Stir in spaghetti sauce.

4. Simmer for 5 minutes.

5. Spread mixture in a 10" x 10" casserole dish.

6. Sprinkle on all the mozzarella cheese and half of the Parmesan cheese.

7. Cover with the crescent rolls; pinch together.

8. Sprinkle with rest of Parmesan cheese.

9. Bake for 15 minutes or until golden brown.

Bug Cookies

Ingredients

Chocolate-covered marshmallow cookies
Black or brown pipe cleaners
White icing
Mini chocolate chips

1. Bend pipe cleaners and push into marshmallow cookie top for legs.

2. Put one spoonful of icing in center of marshmallow cookie.

3. Add mini chocolate chips in the centers for eyes.

94

Every kid should do chores around the house without being paid.

Ginny Ballor
College student
Merrill, MI

Even toddlers can be given small responsibilities around the house. If you can make doing the chores fun, you'll get a lot more cooperation and a lot less whining.

One of the first responsibilities you can give your child is to put toys away. To make this task easier, work with your child to establish a place where everything belongs.

Every six months, cycle your children's toys: move some of them to the closet and bring others out that they haven't seen since the last rotation. Keep those toys that are still fresh, and give away the others.

Provide shelves at your child's height. For young children, don't have more than two shelves high.

Store toys with multiple pieces in clear, plastic tubs on those shelves. Label each tub (use pictures or stickers for children too young to read).

Match size of toy to its container: marbles and jacks in small boxes, medium size for action figures, and so on. This helps children learn where things go.

Choose a corner of the room where your child can keep a puzzle or a Lego project available for easy reach.

When it's time to pick up, set a kitchen timer and challenge your child to beat the clock, picking up all the toys before the buzzer sounds.

Keep a chart on your child's door with those tasks you both have agreed she'll do (make bed, put toys away). Every day at bedtime she gets a star if all the chores are completed. At the end of a week or a month, schedule a celebration if a certain number of stars have been earned.

Help your child dust—instead of using a dust cloth, use a clean mitten or glove whose mate was lost on the playground. Create a dusting buddy by sewing or gluing wiggle eyes, pom-poms, and other features cut out of felt to the back of the mitten or glove. Use glue that can be washed when dry so that the dusting buddy can be cleaned as needed. A mate-less sock also works well if you don't happen to have any extra mittens or gloves.

Make washing the dishes fun. For best results, use translucent dish soap in a see-through bottle. Remove the front label from the bottle. Unscrew the spout and drop in several small, clean, plastic bugs, other small plastic toys, or marbles. When all of the dish soap has been used, remove the objects, wash them, and reward your child for a job well done. Use food coloring to color clear dish soap fun colors.

Kids love to sort, by size, by color, or by shape. The next time you have a basketful of clean socks, let your child sort, match, and pair them. Take a minute when your child isn't looking to make sure that they're paired up correctly—and save yourself from an early-morning headache!

95

Every kid should spend time alone.

Does your child spend free time alone coloring, reading, playing with a favorite toy, or just listening to music? Would your child rather spend that time outside digging in the dirt, studying bugs and flowers and blades of grass, sitting on the swing, or making a million trips up and down the slide? Or does your child constantly bother you for something to do?

Everything around us happens at lightning speed. Email travels around the world in a fraction of a second. We spend a good portion of our time rushing around. Our children are simply a product of the world in which they live.

If your child has a difficult time finding things to do when faced with time alone, spend some time together brainstorming ways to enjoy solitude. Here are some ideas:

- Help your child set up a special spot in his bedroom. Select a comfortable chair, (maybe a beanbag or director's chair) for sitting and listening to music. Make sure that there is adequate lighting for reading, sketching, or journaling. Hang up a few pictures or posters of your child's favorite things.

- Teach your child to play solitaire—a fun way to spend a few minutes alone.

- Buy your child something special with the stipulation that it can only be enjoyed during quiet time in the bedroom. It may be a new book, CD, sketch pad, craft project, or a puzzle; for younger children, maybe a brand-new coloring book and box of crayons, or a special toy. Start slowly, try a few minutes of alone time each day and slowly increase it.

Still bored? If your child claims to have read all the new books, done the puzzle, and finished the craft project, suggest spending some time working on a favorite hobby. Many kids can spend hours alone poring over the details in a favorite hobby.

If your child is still having difficulty spending time alone, consider using a reward chart. Let your child put a star on the chart for every fifteen minutes (or amount of time you determine) spent alone. When a predetermined goal is achieved, it's time for a reward. Consider rewarding a younger child with a watch and time-telling lesson, so that she can keep track of the time spent alone. Start with a digital watch or clock and eventually progress to an analog watch or clock.

96

Every kid should have an adventure.

ad•ven•ture *n* an exciting or remarkable experience

Everyone's idea of an adventure is different. As we grow up and live through different experiences, our view of adventure changes. Your idea of an adventure today is probably vastly different than it was when you were five years old.

To a three- or four-year-old, hiking with Grandpa deep into the woods behind his house might be the idea of an ultimate adventure. At five or six, the ultimate adventure might be the freedom to play in the backyard with Mom or Dad checking up occasionally from the patio door. For a seven- or eight-year-old, adventure might be bike riding with a friend or a first sleepover at a best friend's house. By nine or ten, a weekend camping or fishing with a favorite aunt and uncle might be an adventure. To an eleven- or twelve-year-old, the ultimate adventure might be the dream of hiking to the highest point in each state as a member of the Highpointers Club.

What's your child's idea of the ultimate adventure? If you don't know, discuss it together. While some dreams might be fantastic and unreachable, many of them might be at least partially possible, with a little work and research. For example, a climb to the summit in each state might be impossible, but perhaps your child could get started by climbing to the highest point in your state.

Whatever the adventure, be sure to document the occasion with lots of pictures.

97

Every kid should experience the beauty of nature.

Linda Karaktin
Executive Secretary
Cocoa, FL

Help your child to see the beauty of nature by taking the time to share some or all of these examples:

- The colors of a sunset. Each night, as the sun sets, nature puts on a beautiful display of reds, purples, oranges, and pinks. Put the dinner dishes on hold to catch the show.

- The morning after an ice storm. While the ice-coated roads can be treacherous, that same ice as it coats the limbs of a tree is a spectacular sight as it shimmers in the brilliant sunlight.

- A golden field of wheat, ready for harvest, waving in an autumn breeze.

- A spider, busy at work spinning and weaving her web. If it survives the night, check in the morning for a dew-covered web glistening in the morning sun.

- The first buds of spring.

- A waterfall—the bigger the better. Watch the water cascade down, feel the breeze on your face, and see rainbows dancing in the mist.

- A gentle, nighttime snowfall. Watch the flakes fall from the sky, sparkling like diamond dust in the moonlight.

- Autumn leaves. Check out nature's fiery display in an array of red, yellow, and orange leaves. Keep the memories alive by helping your child press a few leaves between the pages of a large book.

98

Every kid should learn about the family's history.

Your child might know that your family is of German, Irish, or Korean descent, but what about the details? How about the town, county, or region from which your family emigrated? Does your child know how the family came to settle in this country or how they earned a living? Help your child to uncover your family heritage, and maybe learn a little bit about yourself in the process.

The origin of family surnames often began with a traditional occupation—maybe your ancestors were farmers, blacksmiths, or cabinetmakers. Other names were derived from the town or region in which the family lived, or even the first name of the patriarch.

Help your child discover the origins of your family name. If most of your ancestors came from one particular town or country, work with your child to learn as much about that area as possible during the time your ancestors lived there. How did they come to settle in this country, and how did they make a living once they got here? With your child, find out as much as you can about the people on the branches of your family tree.

Start with what you know—your parents, grandparents, and great-grandparents. Get out the family album and linger over each photo, telling all the stories you remember.

Help your child write letters to faraway relatives asking for information.

If it's not too far away, go with your child to research old church records, old gravestones, and old newspaper archives.

The National Archives in Washington, D.C., is a treasure trove of genealogical information. Consider taking your older child on a trip and doing some research, such as reviewing old lists of immigrants coming into Ellis Island.

If your family has a crest, help your child to find out what the symbols represent. Have the family motto translated; how does it fit into the family history? If your family doesn't have a crest, encourage your child to take all the information about your history and create one—complete with a motto. If possible, have the motto translated into the native language of your ancestors.

While you help your child learn about your family heritage, document as much information as you can. Make copies of official documents such as birth certificates, marriage licenses, military documents, and death records, as well as any photographs you find. These will be invaluable if you or your child ever decide to do a detailed study of your family.

99

Every kid should learn the value of  money.

For young children, finding a few pennies on the sidewalk, in a parking lot, or on the floor of a store can turn an ordinary day into a red-letter day. Older children are likely to walk right by those same pennies that thrill and delight young children, unless they have been taught that those few pennies, added to a piggy bank, can eventually buy a pack of trading cards or a small toy.

How you decide to teach your child the value of money will be based on your personal values and beliefs, but here are a few ideas.

If your child gets an allowance, suggest that a portion of the allowance each week should go to your child's favorite charity. By doing this, your child will learn from an early age the importance of helping the less fortunate.

Many families believe another portion should be set aside for savings. To make saving more fun, have your child decorate a large, clean, plastic water or soda bottle. If the mouth of the bottle is too small for nickels and quarters to fit through, use a sharp kitchen or craft knife to cut a slot near the top of the bottle.

Older kids might enjoy using glass paints to personalize and decorate a store-bought ceramic piggy bank. On a regular basis, empty the bottle or bank and help your child deposit the contents in a bank savings account.

To help your child learn more about saving, contact a mutual fund company which sponsors special "young investor" funds. These special funds usually offer kid-friendly coloring books or newsletters aimed at making finances fun. For example, Stein Roe has a Young Investor fund ($1,000 minimum for a custodial account, or $100 with an automatic investment plan of $50 per month requiring a monthly deposit of only $50). In return, the company sends your child quarterly newsletters filled with interesting articles, puzzles, and contests. All of the investments in the fund are dedicated to child-friendly companies, such as McDonald's or Walt Disney. Visit Stein-Roe's website at www.younginvestor.com or call (800)338-2550. The fund is committed to investing 65 percent of its portfolio in stocks that affect the lives of children and teenagers. Stein Roe recently started a new fund, Growth Investor, with holdings identical to Young Investor's but with a lower expense ratio—1.1 percent vs. 1.31

percent—for people who don't want Young Investor's educational materials.

USAA First Start Growth ($250, or $20 a month; (800)235-8377) is the newest fund to be directed toward kids. The fund's prospectus requires it to steer clear of alcohol, tobacco, and gambling stocks, but the funds can be invested in any other companies that are familiar to kids.

Monetta: the seven Monetta funds have minimum initial investments of $250; participants in the youth-investing program called Monetta Express get some special perks. If you open a custodial account and sign up for at least $25 per quarter to be invested automatically, you receive Steady Eddy, a plush bean-filled engine and the first of eight train cars in the Monetta Express (the other seven represent each of the company's funds). Monetta's is the only youth program that offers a money-market fund, Government Money Market (for information, call (800)666-3882).

American Express IDS New Dimensions ($500, or $50 a month with a 5 percent load). New Dimensions already had a thirty-year track record when American Express chose it two years ago as the flagship of its Kids, Parents, and Money program. Call (800) 437-4332 for more information. Like Young Investor, New Dimensions leans toward big, well-known companies. New Dimensions comes with educational materials for kids, including a quarterly newsletter.

Check out the website www.kidsmoney.org for more fun tips on helping kids with money!

100

Every kid should have the opportunity to act like a kid.

Kelly McCoy
College student
Rochester Hills, MI

The days of childhood are short. Every child should be allowed to act like a kid as often as possible, and:

- Walk barefoot during a summer rain, squishing mud between her toes.

- Jump on the bed.

- Roll down a hill.

- Eat dessert first once in a while.

- Go to the zoo and imitate the animals.

- Make goofy faces.

- Splash in the puddles after a spring rain.

- Eat too many cookies before dinner.

- Spin, until they can spin no more, and then fall down on the grass.

- Sing loud and off-key.

- Go on a picnic in the park.

- Slurp ice cream.

- Celebrate the start of the school year with a brand-new box of crayons.

- Walk in snowdrifts.

- Play in the rain.

- "Ice skate" around the living room on sheets of waxed paper.

- Have a snowball fight.

- Wish on dandelions gone to seed.

101

Every kid should have a dream for the future and an adult who believes in that dream.

Firefighter...Teacher...Astronaut...Doctor...Police officer...Ballerina...
Race car driver...Super hero...Actor...Professional basketball player...
Rock star...Artist...Pilot...Private eye...President of the United States...

Every child has a dream for the future; who he would like to be, or what she wants to do as an adult. And, no matter how far-fetched the dream might seem, remember that at one time, the person your child hopes to emulate, whether it be a doctor, actor, rock star, or President of the United States, was a child with a dream.

Help your child explore the dream, no matter what it is. With your child, discover what it will take to make the dream a reality. Investigate what kinds of skills or education are needed to be successful. Remind your child that very rarely does success come without a lot of hard work, determination, and failures along the way.

Try to find someone working in the field or specific job in which your child is interested. Set up a meeting for your child to talk to the person about his or her profession; the reality of it, good *and* bad, and, if possible, a day (or part of a day) of job shadowing. Make a few phone calls on your child's behalf and see what you can arrange. You might be surprised how willing people are to help children learn about their profession.

For the child who wants more than anything to be Superman or Wonder Woman, explore realistic options—maybe a police officer, firefighter, or paramedic, all of whom help people in need, just like Superman and Wonder Woman.

It's OK if your child's dreams and aspirations do not resemble the dreams that you have for him or her. Don't try to trim your child's hopes to fit your own ideas. Accept them as is. And, above all, always encourage your child to reach for the stars, and to dare to dream!

CHECKLIST

Every kid should...

❏   1. Do something to make the world a better place

❏   2. Believe in things that can't be seen

❏   3. Go outside at dusk and stay there until it's dark, watching the stars come out

❏   4. Camp in the backyard

❏   5. Play in the bathtub until his skin wrinkles

❏   6. Play with play dough

❏   7. Receive notes of support, encouragement, or "just because"

❏   8. Catch snowflakes on his tongue and eyelashes

❏   9. Write a thank-you note of gratitude to a relative or teacher

❏ 10. Own one really fun piece of clothing

❏ 11. Turn off the television for a weekend

❏ 12. Eat homemade ice cream on a hot summer evening

- [ ] 13. Help create a scrapbook of her childhood memories
- [ ] 14. Go to a museum
- [ ] 15. Build a gingerbread house and then get to eat it
- [ ] 16. Spit watermelon seeds
- [ ] 17. Do a "senior study"
- [ ] 18. Receive praise for who she is and what she has accomplished
- [ ] 19. Have a favorite book or bedtime story
- [ ] 20. Take a nighttime hike by the light of the moon
- [ ] 21. Receive an award
- [ ] 22. Make a special homemade present for Mom or Dad, Grandpa or Grandma
- [ ] 23. Express creativity
- [ ] 24. Learn how to swim
- [ ] 25. Go for a ride in a small airplane
- [ ] 26. Experiment with simple science projects
- [ ] 27. Take music lessons
- [ ] 28. Help bake a cake from scratch and then lick the frosting bowl

❑ 29. Grow a vegetable garden

❑ 30. Blow a bubble gum bubble until it pops

❑ 31. Experience a family car trip

❑ 32. See a classic movie on the big screen

❑ 33. Go to a parade

❑ 34. Write in a journal

❑ 35. Create a holiday keepsake

❑ 36. Participate in a "-thon"

❑ 37. Possess a soft, cuddly stuffed animal, that he is never forced to give up because he's "too old"

❑ 38. Have a collection

❑ 39. Attend a live performance

❑ 40. Let a fuzzy caterpillar crawl up her arm, and then watch that caterpillar turn into a butterfly

❑ 41. Create a self-portrait

❑ 42. Build a sand castle in the summer and a snow fort in the winter

❑ 43. Go on a factory tour

❑ 44. Decorate the driveway

❑ 45. Write a "memory letter" each year

- ❏ 46. Explore other cultures
- ❏ 47. Play dress-up
- ❏ 48. Eat green eggs
- ❏ 49. Ride a horse
- ❏ 50. Have a treasure box
- ❏ 51. Spend some time on a farm, even for a short visit
- ❏ 52. Be allowed the freedom to make choices, decisions, and mistakes
- ❏ 53. Go to a fair, carnival, or amusement park
- ❏ 54. Visit the place(s) where Mom and Dad grew up
- ❏ 55. Get dressed up and go to a fancy dinner or restaurant
- ❏ 56. Create a board game
- ❏ 57. Have one outstanding teacher
- ❏ 58. Write a letter to a favorite actor, athlete, or hero
- ❏ 59. Have a pet
- ❏ 60. Have a hobby
- ❏ 61. Decorate her room according to the theme of her choice

- ❑ 62. Take a trip to Washington, D.C.
- ❑ 63. Have a secret hideout
- ❑ 64. Play classic games
- ❑ 65. Run a lemonade stand
- ❑ 66. Mark birthdays with a celebration
- ❑ 67. Clown around
- ❑ 68. Go to a family reunion
- ❑ 69. Make a pizza
- ❑ 70. Learn to appreciate the different abilities of people
- ❑ 71. Be taken for a "pajama ride"
- ❑ 72. Have a "get better" box
- ❑ 73. Blow soap bubbles
- ❑ 74. Spend some time alone with each parent
- ❑ 75. Build a model
- ❑ 76. Go on a scavenger hunt
- ❑ 77. Go to a baseball game with Grandpa
- ❑ 78. Play with his food
- ❑ 79. See Mom or Dad laugh
- ❑ 80. Make caramel apples
- ❑ 81. Publish a book

- ❏ 82. Have a best friend
- ❏ 83. Experience the feelings of love, safety, and security
- ❏ 84. Participate in an extracurricular activity
- ❏ 85. Have a pen pal
- ❏ 86. Have a personal library card
- ❏ 87. Enjoy lazy summer days
- ❏ 88. Experience the ocean
- ❏ 89. Be given a camera to take pictures, and the freedom to take whatever pictures she wants to take
- ❏ 90. Produce a video
- ❏ 91. Experience the mystery of magic
- ❏ 92. Go to summer camp
- ❏ 93. Make a meal for the family
- ❏ 94. Do chores around the house without being paid
- ❏ 95. Spend time alone
- ❏ 96. Have an adventure
- ❏ 97. Experience the beauty of nature
- ❏ 98. Learn about the family's history
- ❏ 99. Learn the value of money

❑ 100. Have the opportunity to act like a kid
❑ 101. Have a dream for the future and an adult who
     believes in that dream

BE A KID!

About the Author

Alecia T. Devantier is a former educator with a master's degree in teaching. She has worked on a national curriculum development program and organized and conducted numerous workshops on the use of technology in the classroom. She served as a contributing writer for *HomeWords* magazine and website, and wrote about family issues, educational topics, and crafts. Some of the ideas for this collection have been provided by experts from around the country: parents, grandparents, educators, child care providers, and the kids themselves.